The American House

The American House

ROBIN LANGLEY SOMMER

Thunder Bay
P·R·E·S·S

Page 1: The exuberant Queen Anne Revival-style Donnelly House (1893), Mount Dora, Florida.

Page 2: Pfeiffer's Homestead, Grand Teton National Park, Wyoming.

Page 3: Antique plaque indicating payment of Philadelphia's Fire Tax.

Below: Entrance Hall, Rosedown, St. Francisville, Louisiana.

Published in the United States by
Thunder Bay Press
An imprint of the Advantage
Publishers Group
5880 Oberlin Drive, Suite 400
San Diego, CA 92121-4794
http://www.advantagebooksonline.com

Produced by Saraband Inc., PO Box 0032, Rowayton, CT 06853-0032

Copyright © 2000 Saraband Inc

Design © Ziga Design

THIS BOOK IS DEDICATED TO
DEBBY AND ED COOPER.

ISBN 1-57145-283-4

Library of Congress Cataloging-in-Publication Data available upon request.

1 2 3 4 5 6 7 8 9 10

Contents

Introduction   6

1. English Colonial Styles   24

2. European Influences   54

3. Frontier and Folk Housing   80

4. Mansions, Estates, and Plantations   110

5. Vernacular Styles   144

6. The Victorian Era   180

7. Early Modernism   220

Glossary   252

Bibliography   253

Index   254

Acknowledgments   256

Photo Credits   256

Introduction

Previous pages:
The gold-mining
ghost town of Bodie,
California.

As one of our basic needs, shelter has much to tell us about a nation's history, culture, social concerns, commerce, fads, and fashions. The story of the North American house is especially rich and varied because of the many different ethnic groups who have influenced our residential architecture from the early 1600s to the present day. This volume focuses on the period between the early days of European settlement in the New World, primarily by colonists from England, France, Sweden, Germany, and the Netherlands, and the inception of Modern architecture, as influenced by Louis Sullivan, Frank Lloyd Wright, and other brilliant men and women who saw living space in new ways and shaped our ideas accordingly. From the early twentieth century onward, Old World designers began looking to the United States for inspiration—a complete reversal of previous patterns—and gifted architects from Europe and the Far East helped forge new syntheses that increasingly reflect the multicultural concept of the global village.

The English Colonial styles are the first that spring to mind when we reflect upon the earliest period of East Coast settlement, from Jamestown, Virginia, to the Massachusetts Bay Colony. The latter enclave was founded by persecuted dissenters from the established Church of England—the Puritans—while Jamestown, in the Chesapeake Bay or Tidewater region, was primarily a commercial enterprise (and none too successful in its earliest days). The two regions shared similar building styles that evolved from the medieval cottages, farmsteads, and towns of the Mother Country, but climatic differences were apparent in the types of shelter constructed. Stylistic differences would become more marked as the Northern colonies became more urbanized and the Southern colonies moved further into a plantation-based economy.

As the Eastern Seaboard colonies prospered through maritime trade and the growth of domestic agriculture and industry, they moved from relatively crude housing, often based on Native American

*Right: The medieval-
style Iron Master's
House (1646) at
Saugus Ironworks
National Historic
Site, Massachusetts.*

models, toward more spacious and comfortable dwellings based on English architecture, from Jacobean to Georgian, Adam, and Regency styles. After the Revolutionary War, the emergent Federal style, including Jeffersonian Classicism, reflected a departure from imitation of English models that was consistent with the new sense of national identity and autonomy. Building materials reflected regional availability and innovations based on climate, topography, and vernacular styles. In Eastern Canada (formerly New France) the Georgian style became ascendant after the British conquest of 1763.

Wood—so plentiful in the New World as compared to the long-populated British Isles—was the primary construction material, followed by brick and stone, whether rough fieldstone gathered from cleared farmland, or native granite, limestone, sandstone, and other quarried masonry. Timber construction of the traditional post-and-beam kind was widely prevalent well into the nineteenth century. As Frank E. Wallis observes in *Colonial Homes in the Southern States* (Arno Press, 1977): "Our Colonial, the son of the Georgian, has clapboards, porches in Doric and Corinthian or near Corinthian, cornices, and modillions, or cornices ornamented with the invention of our own native joiners; for wood to these old men was a servant, and they played in and out through the grain of the woods for their curves and their applied ornaments." The carpenter was not only a master craftsman, but a designer as well, freely interpreting from pattern books and building manuals before there were any professional architects as we know them.

As the English colonies became more affluent, the Georgian style of the Mother

Country remained pre-eminent for both housing and public buildings. It was based on classical design principles as interpreted by the Italian architect Andrea de Pietro, known as Palladio. In 1570 he had published his influential *Quattro Libri* (*Four Books on Architecture*), which inspired a Classical revival in England and, later, in North America. The hallmarks of this late-Renaissance style include detailing based on Classical Greek and Roman models; windows with rounded, or Palladian, heads; and ornamental doorways surmounted by pediments (later, fan-shaped windows called fanlights). The doorway was often flanked by engaged flattened columns, or pilasters, that projected from the façade. It might also have

Above: A cupola, or belvedere, crowning Mount Vernon, George Washington's historic Virginia estate house.

Above: Handmade shutters and rough siding on a Southeastern folk house (c. 1820).

and James Adam brought a lighter touch to town and country houses along the Eastern Seaboard. Robert Adam traveled to Italy to observe Classical architecture firsthand and introduced new and graceful forms of ornamentation including urns, swags, and garlands.

Many features of the English Georgian interior found their way into North American homes and have remained influential in Colonial Revival styles to the present day. Symmetrical façades with restrained Classical ornamentation opened onto central-hall plans that might include molded-plaster ceiling decorations; spiral staircases; wainscoting in oak or mahogany; triangular and broken pediments over doorways; figured wallpaper; and fireplaces with fluted pilasters and dentiled cornices (carved with regular tooth-shaped indentations). In some examples, paneling above the mantel carried the fireplace almost as high as the ceiling moldings.

What is now New England is especially rich in Georgian- and Federal-style mansions built by affluent merchants, sea captains, and landholders. Boston and Salem, Massachusetts, and the Rhode Island cities of Newport and Providence, have handsome examples of the style, as illustrated in chapter 1. The Tidewater region, radiating outward from the original settlement at Jamestown, Virginia (1607), is a microcosm of the evolution of Southern estate-house styles, from the Jacobean to the Greek Revival. Substantial brick or stone townhouses have been preserved in such Seaboard cities as Quebec, Boston, Philadelphia, and Alexandria, Virginia. Regional differences are apparent in the facts that the Southern house often had a large central dormer, flanked by two or more smaller ones, and a kitchen separate

narrow windows on either side and a rounded or squared portico, which protected the entrance from the elements and emphasized the centrally placed doorway.

The Georgian style flourished in England between about 1650 and 1750, under the auspices of such architects as Inigo Jones, Christopher Wren, and James Gibbs. It reached the height of its influence in the future United States before the Revolutionary War, but many of its features were carried through and modified in the Federal style that gained ascendancy under the influence of president and architect Thomas Jefferson. About 1800 the elegant Classical style named for the English architects Robert

from the main house because of the long hot summers. Colder climates dictated both steeper rooflines to shed snow efficiently and tighter insulation.

Of course, the vast majority of Colonial settlers in North America lived on a modest scale. Their vernacular architecture was originally based on postmedieval models, characterized by an overhanging second story called a jetty, thatched or shingled roofs designed to shed rain and snow, large stacked chimneys, and small casement windows, often diamond-paned. The jetty added structural stability to the timber-framed house, and the windows had small panes because glass—where available—was expensive until the early 1800s, when improved glazing techniques were imported from Europe. Most windows and some doors had shutters that could be closed during bad weather. It was not until the mid-nineteenth century that window sashes were regularly glazed in larger units, leading to the prevalence of the double-hung sash window that we know today and the displacement of the casement window, except in certain regional or revival styles.

Chimneys, which played a vital role in heating and ventilation, dispersed cooking odors when the fireplace was the "kitchen stove," usually located in the common room accessed through the front door. Prior to the introduction of the chimney in the late Middle Ages, smoke had escaped from the house through small openings in the attic roof. When chimneys came into use, second stories could be floored and attics used for additional living or storage space. In early North American houses, most chimneys were built of wood and clay—a dangerous fire hazard—or of locally made brick,

fieldstone, or a combination of these materials. The Southern colonies tended to place their chimneys outside the house, on one or both of the gable walls, while interior chimneys were preferred in the Northeast and Canada. The exception was Rhode Island, where massive exterior stone chimneys comprised most of one gable end. These houses were called "stone-enders," and appeared as early as 1640. The Atlantic Coast "saltbox" house, so called for its resemblance to a medieval salt cellar, was a variation of the stone-ender. It was expanded as families grew by a lean-to addition at the back, usually comprising a separate kitchen, with its own chimney; a "borning room" for the

Below: A graceful wrought-iron railing and lantern at the Owens-Thomas House (1817), on Oglethorpe Square, in Savannah, Georgia.

care of newborns and the sick or elderly; and a pantry. Sometimes the house was extended a second time, so that the roof on the back reached almost to the ground. Many houses were designed with the steeply sloping roof on the north, or "weather" side, which was then banked with straw or other materials for winter insulation. Residents of Eastern Canada's Atlantic Provinces also built in this style.

Most early New England dwellings were one room deep and two stories high, built on an I-shaped plan with a central chimney. Later, paired chimneys would become common, usually placed at the gable ends. Single-story houses were modeled on the English hall-and-parlor plan, "hall" referring to the common room rather than the passageway we think of today. Both types were framed in timber joined by hand-hewn notches and covered with clapboards or shingles for weatherproofing. The New England garrison house had

an overhanging second story and, like the stone-ender, was often expanded by a lean-to addition at the back.

Local conditions, like the shifting sand on Massachusetts' Cape Cod, were met with ingenious solutions. As Lester Walker points out in *American Shelter* (Overlook Press, 1981): "Early Cape Cod cottages were built by ship's carpenters as though they were 'land boats' made to ride shifting sands and withstand lashing wind and rain storms; they were low and broad, averaging twenty-five by forty feet, with only a seven-foot ceiling height. They were built on large hewn oak sills, which steadied the house on its shifting uneven sand site. [They] had no projections or exterior extraneous decoration, so they could resist ocean gale forces." Inside, the rooms were grouped around a huge chimney containing up to four fireplaces. Numerous tiny bedrooms occupied the attic story, each with its own small window.

Right: A French-Canadian country house with flaring eaves under snow in Rosemere, Quebec.

During the 1600s, immigrants from several European countries, notably Sweden, the Netherlands, and Germany, brought their own distinctive building styles to the New World. Swedish colonists of the Delaware Valley region used timber-framing techniques from their homeland to build log "cribs" or cabins, usually one-room structures in which the log walls were joined at the corners by various types of notching. Early log cabins, which were widely imitated by settlers from other countries, usually consisted of undressed timbers (with their original bark) and split-log rafters covered with cedar shingles, which were highly weather resistant. A stone fireplace protruded from the gable end of the dwelling, and the chimney was built of sticks and mud, which posed the threat of hidden chimney fires. Often two log cribs were roofed over by a single span, leaving a passageway between them. They would become known as dogtrot cabins, with the open passage used as a wagon pass-through where one of the cribs served as a stable or crop storage area.

German immigrants, too, brought log-building traditions from south-central Europe. Called *Fachwerk*, their timber-framing techniques were used to raise sturdy farmhouses and barns in the mid-Atlantic colonies of Pennsylvania, New Jersey, Delaware, and Maryland. Early houses consisted of simple single-room plans with an exterior chimney of brick or stone. More elaborate Continental log houses might have three rooms served by a central chimney. The Germans also built timber-framed masonry houses, barns, and mills, of which examples have been preserved due to the durability of the materials and the strength of the timber framing.

Scots-Irish immigrants, who were skilled in masonry building techniques, also played an important role in the Delaware Valley region, and the culture that developed there was spreading along three migratory routes by about 1700: westward into Pennsylvania, southwestward along the Appalachians, and south to the Carolinas.

The Dutch East India Company brought settlers from the Netherlands during the early 1600s, and the Dutch Colonial style became prevalent in New York's Hudson River Valley, New Jersey, Long Island, and what is now New York City (originally New Amsterdam). Dutch farmers and merchants built one-and-one-half-story houses of stone and timber with brick veneering. Early townhouses rose in Albany, New Amsterdam, Kingston (originally Wittwyck), and Schenectady, New York, one or two stories high and

Above: *Montreal's historic Pierre du Calvet House (1725), an exemplar of the Quebec style.*

several rooms deep. Many of them had stepped or curvilinear Flemish gables, and brick veneering was applied to the street side to conform to the fire laws, although the other three sides, with their wooden cladding, might be left exposed. Brick was made by hand from local clay, and its quality and availability made for regional differences in color, ranging from yellow and buff to the familiar red. Townhouses overlooked narrow cobbled streets and showed their medieval lineage in their steeply pitched parapeted rooflines and paired end chimneys. Farther inland, houses of coursed stone gleaned from the fields were more common.

The two-sloped roof often attributed to the Dutch was probably, in fact, an adaptation of the gambrel roof developed in England to provide more storage in the attic or loft area. Much later, the gambrel roof would be a feature of neo-Dutch Colonial housing, as seen from Long Island to western Pennsylvania. It is most closely identified with North American barns, of which it became characteristic. The Dutch culture area in the Hudson River Valley remained static because of its conquest by the English in 1664. While New Englanders migrated northward into Maine and westward across New York State, Dutch influence dwindled except in the original areas of settlement.

The powerful French presence in North America from the early 1600s onward influenced architecture from Eastern Canada down to the Mississippi Valley. French settlers of Quebec were known as *habitants* — those who came to stay, as distinct from the traders, trappers, missionaries, and military personnel who built few settlements apart from stockades and usually returned to their native country after terms of service in what was then New France. Houses built in the French style were mainly single-story buildings with narrow door and window openings flanked by shutters. Originally, steeply pitched roofs were the norm, especially where snowload was a factor. Over time, the four-sided hipped roof gained favor. Walls were often of stucco over half-timbered frames. In low-lying areas, the house was raised on posts to prevent flooding, with access to the main level by outside stairways. This style became prevalent near the mouth of the Mississippi, where flooding was a regular occurrence and intricate bayous provided a refuge to French-speaking Acadians expelled from Eastern Canada by the British. The "Cajuns" became a distinct ethnic and cultural group in southern Louisiana and remain so to the present day.

Examples of the French-style urban cottage, predating the Louisiana Purchase of 1803, may still be seen in parts of New Orleans, although most have been altered significantly. The typical cottage fronted directly onto the street, without the porch that would become a dominant feature of American architecture. The roof was usually side-gabled and had flaring, or bell-cast, eaves. In rural areas, the French colonists built timber-framed masonry houses with steeply pitched hipped roofs, or log houses of the *pièce-sur-pièce* type, with walling slotted into upright posts on a rot-resistant sill, or footing.

The Spanish presence was most influential in Florida and the present-day Southwest, including California. In fact, apart from Taos Pueblo, New Mexico, St. Augustine, Florida, is the nation's oldest city, founded in 1565. There are deep affinities between Native American construction methods using adobe (mud)

bricks made with straw and Spanish buildings of adobe, as introduced from North Africa by the Moors. The first crude huts at St. Augustine were gradually replaced by single-story dwellings with asymmetrical façades and tiled roofs, usually built around a patio or courtyard for privacy and coolness. Thick walls of adobe brick, rubblestone, or native shellstone were usually covered with stucco, or, in the Southwest, with puddled (liquid) adobe—a weather-resistant coating that protected the structure and was renewed regularly. Native American construction methods were freely adapted by Spanish colonists to their own style, with arches, colonnades, and courtyards in houses and public buildings. Timber roof supports, called *vigas*, protrude from the façades of Spanish Colonial houses and from the Pueblo and other Revival-style dwellings that followed. Hooded masonry fireplaces indoors served for heating and cooking purposes, as did the beehive-shaped adobe ovens outside the house in many Hispanic communities.

Frontier and folk housing modeled on various building traditions spread west and south of the Chesapeake Bay culture area originating at Jamestown, and by the early eighteenth century, what we may call the first frontier had reached into the Midwest and the Deep South. It was in the early American heartland that various regional and ethnic styles mixed to form the first truly national culture area. Homesteaders borrowed ideas and techniques for house building from one another to create recognizably American dwellings even before the Revolutionary War. These would evolve into vernacular adaptations as westward migration and settlement extended from the Ohio River Valley to the Pacific Coast during the nineteenth century. The log cabin, in various forms, became identified with the frontier east of the Mississippi River, where wood remained the primary building material. Railroads, canals, riverboats, turnpikes, and other transportation networks developed to expedite settlement of the trans-Mississippi West, where

Above: The Pittock Mansion in Portland, Oregon, constructed in 1914 in the imposing Chateauesque style.

homesteaders faced new challenges in the form of climatic extremes on the Great Plains. Wood was scarce there, and housing was built of sod carved from the prairie. Long, bitter winters and hot summers took their toll on these shelters, whose sod roofs on pole frameworks often leaked and sometimes collapsed.

The Rocky Mountains posed a formidable challenge to settlement of the Pacific Coast, including the Northwest, but determined railroad engineers, stagecoach lines, and wagonmasters made their way through, and the growing transportation system made building materials more available to emerging towns from St. Louis to San Francisco. The advent of sawmills, factory-made bricks, and rapid balloon framing with boards precut to standard lengths facilitated the building boom. With many regional variations, as described in chapters 3 and 5, the

North American house continued to evolve rapidly, from the miner's shack of wood and tarpaper to the Anglo-Spanish ranch houses of Cattle Kingdom days.

Long before this, wealthy merchants, planters, and landholders had built the nation's first mansions, estates, and plantation houses along the Atlantic Seaboard, from Maine to Virginia. In Waltham, Massachusetts, Salem architect Samuel McIntire designed the Lyman Estate, called The Vale, in 1793. This handsome Federal-style house had extensive grounds laid out on eighteenth-century English design principles. Its historic greenhouses reflect the passion for horticulture displayed from the earliest days of the Republic and fostered by gentleman farmers like Thomas Jefferson, who traveled extensively in Europe as a statesman, and George Washington, who spent most of a lifetime improving his family property at

Mount Vernon, Virginia—perhaps the nation's best-known residence, followed closely by Jefferson's Monticello.

Providence, Rhode Island, now the second-largest New England city after Boston, has several excellent eighteenth-century houses built a century before nearby Newport became a fashionable resort for wealthy New Yorkers. About 1792 Colonel Joseph Nightingale built a three-story wooden mansion with bevelled quoins of cut stone to delineate the corners. Its central-hall plan would remain predominant in the region well into the 1800s. An unusual example of late-Renaissance Jacobean detailing appears on the Christopher Arnold House (c. 1735), with its overhanging gable below a hipped roof. The Jacobean style was also used for some of the earliest Southern manor houses, laid out in cruciform plans and distinguished by high end walls with stepped or curved gables and tall three-part chimneys serving multiple fireplaces.

In Maine, the historic Hamilton House (c. 1785) was built in the late Georgian style on a site overlooking the Salmon River. Purchased by Emily and Elise Tyson a hundred years later, it was restored to its original beauty, with landscaped formal gardens, elegant murals, and antique furnishings. Ships' captains and large landholders built impressive houses along the coast, which would be followed in the nineteenth century by the luxurious vacation homes of businessmen and financiers.

Below: A romantic nineteenth-century "Moravian Castle," part of an extensive indoor/outdoor museum near Doylestown, Pennsylvania.

Colonial New Castle, Delaware, was an important Delaware Valley enclave dating back to the time of New Sweden and New Netherland. Many handsome townhouses remain here, including the Amstel House, a three-story brick house built about 1730 with a wide gable and Dutch-style detailing. It shares features of the substantial Colonial townhouses now seen mainly in Boston, Philadelphia, and Alexandria,

Below: One of Savannah's many delightful townhouses, with tall hooded windows, Classical entryway, and delicate filigree balustrade.

Virginia. The latter city is especially rich in historic houses, including Fairfax House on Cameron Street; Carlyle House (1745), which is now part of the Braddock Hotel and was built by a friend of George Washington's; and Colross House (1799), with wings added in 1850. All three are of brick construction with stone trim and Georgian detailing.

As the plantation economy of the South expanded, with slave labor imported to grow crops like rice and tobacco, then cotton and sugar cane, the Southern plantation house took form from the James River to the Mississippi. Most of the crops were transported by riverboat, and the houses were located on hilltop sites near the waterways for coolness. Large porches, often supported by columns, provided good ventilation and views of the surrounding grounds on holdings that ranged from hundreds to thousands of acres. Early in the nineteenth century, the newly popular Greek Revival style was used for many of these estate houses. Those constructed along the lower Mississippi delta were influenced by Creole architecture, combining French and West Indian influences.

As westward migration continued apace, new estates were built in a variety of nineteenth-century Revival styles, including the Gothic in its many picturesque incarnations; the ubiquitous Greek Revival; and Victorian-era introductions including the eclectic Queen Anne, Stick style, Italianate, Swiss Chalet, and Renaissance Revival. Mansions in the briefly popular Octagon style had their day, as did the products of the Exotic Revival, inspired by Egyptian, Moorish, and other Near Eastern prototypes. American architects trained in Paris, beginning with Richard Morris

Hunt, brought the eclectic Beaux Arts style, based on Classical forms elaborated with lavish ornamentation in a variety of Renaissance modes, to the national scene. Hunt's work is seen in such Newport, Rhode Island, mansions as Marble House (1892) and The Breakers, designed for Cornelius Vanderbilt II in 1895. The influential New York firm of McKim, Mead, and White executed many commissions in this style, and also contributed to the widespread Colonial Revival that extended well into the twentieth century through their firsthand studies of Classical Georgian houses in the New England states.

The Spanish Colonial Revival style flourished in parts of the Southwest, much of California, and, later, in Florida, when it became accessible by rail and was developed as a wealthy resort area. Eastlake, Richardsonian Romanesque, the Tudor Revival, and Chateauesque all figured in the rich tapestry of country houses and urban landmarks nationwide, which are described and illustrated in chapter 4.

Of course, many modest interpretations of these various styles began to appear across the continent as the population grew and clusters of sparse settlement became towns and cities. The Victorian era brought a new emphasis on the picturesque, as advocated by such influential architects as Alexander Jackson Davis, who embraced the Gothic Revival style imported from England during the 1830s. Closely allied with Davis was Andrew Jackson Downing, a prolific writer and landscape designer. Downing's book *Cottage Residences*, published in 1842, offered middle-income alternatives to Gothic Revival stone mansions like Davis's Lyndhurst, in Tarrytown, New York (1838), with their expensive stone tracery

and asymmetrical plans designed for large sites. Downing published affordable plans for "cottage-villas in a rural Gothic style" that could be executed in wood. They looked back to medieval days with their diamond-paned windows, angular brick chimneys with ornamental chimney pots, and scroll-sawn bargeboards outlining steeply pitched gables. This elaborate wooden detailing took the place of tracery carved from stone, and it became more intricate and profuse as the nineteenth century wore on, resulting in such specialized forms as Carpenter's Gothic, Steamboat Gothic, and the richly embellished High Victorian Gothic and Queen Anne styles.

Houses, schools, and churches in various Gothic forms sprang up to contrast with the classical Greek Revival style, which had been the reigning mode since about 1825. Americans had taken this style to their hearts because it was based directly on such models as the Parthenon at Athens (432 BC), which was—rightly or wrongly—associated with democracy. The Classical form given to the nation's new capital at Washington, D.C., by architects Benjamin Latrobe, Robert Mills, James Hoban, and others was another major influence. Columned porticoes and simple pediments and friezes were added to modest vernacular houses with the aid of carpenters' and builders' manuals. Sometimes they were combined freely with Roman features, including domes, which had been introduced by Thomas Jefferson in his designs for the Virginia State Capitol at Richmond (1786), and the University of Virginia at Charlottesville—among the major achievements in American architecture. Early essays in the Romanesque style would be reprised in the late nineteenth century, primarily under the auspices of architect Henry Hobson Richardson, whose name became associated with an indigenous style using massive rounded arches with deeply recessed entryways and short powerful stone or wooden piers rather than tall slender columns. Romanesque forms influenced Shingle-style architecture, especially in fashionable resort communities, and were emulated by Frank Lloyd Wright early in his career, as seen in many turn-of-the-century buildings in and around Oak Park, Illinois, which was the site of his first home/studio.

Other popular styles of the mid- to late 1800s were the Italianate and the French Second Empire. Writer A.J. Downing's *Architecture of Country Houses* included

Below: The festive Queen Anne-style Holly Hill House in Avalon, on Santa Catalina Island, California.

a "Villa in the Italian style," for which the British-American architect Richard Upjohn had designed the prototype in 1845. Rambling Tuscan-style villas and cubical Italianate townhouses with bracketed cornices were enormously popular before the Civil War. Italianate brownstones (actually brick houses faced with sandstone, with adapted Renaissance detailing) lined lower Manhattan's fashionable Gramercy Park and advanced for blocks along Fifth Avenue. This became the city's most desirable residential address when 840-acre Central Park was completed by landscape architect Frederick Law Olmsted and architect Calvert Vaux.

Italianate detailing was often combined with the French Second Empire style, ushered in by Napoleon III and Baron Georges-Eugène Haussmann, Prefect of the Seine, who made immense municipal improvements to the city of Paris during the emperor's mid-century reign. New boulevards were created, lined with mansard-roofed houses (having four steep sides inset with large dormer windows in elaborate frames). The style had been popularized by the seventeenth-century French architect François Mansart, who established Classicism in French Baroque architecture, and it was widely emulated in North America before and after the Civil War. The mansard roof, whether its slopes were convex, concave, or S-shaped, provided additional living space for growing families and added elegance, height, and harmony to domestic architecture from Montreal to Savannah, Georgia.

The Arts and Crafts movement, which has enjoyed a strong revival of interest in recent years, was a major influence on North American architecture and decorative arts during the late nineteenth and

early twentieth centuries. It originated in Great Britain among architects who were dissatisfied with strict Gothic Revival forms for domestic architecture and with the machine-made, mass-produced products formerly made by hand with care and craftsmanship. British architects including Philip Webb, Eden Nesfield, and Richard Norman Shaw looked toward the "Old English" vernacular of the Jacobean, Elizabethan, and Tudor eras. A cofounder of the movement was designer William Morris, for whom Webb designed the famous Red House in Bexleyheath, Kent (1859). Gifted and idealistic, the proponents of the movement spread their gospel to North America with the help of architect Charles F.A. Voysey. Here, it was espoused not only by the earliest Modern architects, including Frank Lloyd Wright and Charles and Henry Greene, but by the creators of art pottery, Mission-style

furniture, decorative textiles, and a host of other objects that adhered to Morris's dictum: "Have nothing in your houses that you do not know to be useful, or believe to be beautiful."

Wright's mentor was Louis Henri Sullivan, whose work in and around Chicago led him to be acclaimed as the first great Modern American architect after his death in 1924. His rich ornamentation was based on natural forms, and although he is best known for his pioneering skyscrapers, his residential commissions, including Chicago's Charnley House (1891), embodied the spacious living areas, burnished woodwork and the leaded art glass that would become characteristic of Wright's innovative early period. Wright's Prairie-style houses were identifiable by cleanly defined horizontal planes and interior spaces that flowed into one another, the structure rising from the site as an organic whole, with an integral relationship between indoor and outdoor "rooms." He experimented boldly with new construction techniques and materials, including poured concrete, atrium-style glazed roofing, extensive use of exterior banding (beltcourses) to emphasize the horizontal, and concrete block cast in ornamental forms, which he called "textile blocks." His masterful use of ornamentation combined the Arts and Crafts ethos with the use of high-quality machine-made products, resulting eventually in his livable and affordable Usonian houses of the 1930s and '40s.

Below: Vickridge, in Colorado Springs, is a handsome essay in Southwestern Modernism.

Other American exponents of the Arts and Crafts style included several Utopian communities established along lines laid down in England by historian John Ruskin, author of *The Stones of Venice* and *The Seven Lamps of Architecture*, during the mid-1800s. These communities included Roycroft, in East Aurora, New York, and Rose Valley, New York, where craftsmen lived and worked together in a manner reminiscent of the medieval guild, earning modest wages for their furniture, metalwork, and bookbinding. Rose Valley architect William Price designed a house for Edward Bok, publisher of *The Ladies' Home Journal*, who was instrumental in spreading Wright's ideas on attractive, affordable housing.

The Arts and Crafts movement gained momentum with the advent of the enterprising Gustav Stickley, trained as an architect, who established his Craftsman furniture plant in Syracuse, New York, in 1898. His design publication *The Craftsman* reached a wide audience, providing mail-order plans for inexpensive bungalow-style houses (called "Craftsman Homes") and advertisements for his unadorned Mission-style furnishings, made of solid oak finished and stained by hand. In their simplicity of design and good craftsmanship, they recalled the handiwork of the rapidly dwindling Shaker communities, who had lived a communal lifestyle based on spiritual principles since their immigration from England in the early 1800s.

The Greene brothers, Charles and Henry, were especially influential in the California Arts and Crafts movement, with their landmark designs for "the ultimate bungalow," including the 12,000-square-foot Robert R. Blacker house in

Pasadena. Pictured in a 1909 edition of *House Beautiful*, the long, low structure is a recently restored masterpiece of wood joinery, art glass, and Eastern details including second-story sleeping porches with Japanese-style railings. Like Wright, the Greenes insisted upon integrating house with site and coordinating furnishings and appointments to the smallest detail. Some twenty-five masterworks by Greene & Greene are extant in California, including the Gamble House, now in the hands of the University of Southern California at Los Angeles.

The Art Deco style imported from Europe during the 1920s was more often employed for commercial centers like hotels, cinemas, and skyscrapers than for housing. However, the streamlined Art Moderne style became popular for domestic architecture between 1920 and World War II. It combined smooth stucco façades with rounded corners, flat roofs with low parapets, and the use of glass blocks as window and wall ornamentation. The Art Moderne house was influenced by the new look in automobiles, trains, and airplanes and served as an architectural expression of the machine age. Part of the emerging International Style movement, it was identifiably American in its focus on functionalism, from stainless-steel window and door trim to rounded toasters, refrigerators, and kitchen stoves.

Several Early Modern architects came from Europe to live and work in the United States, including Eliel Saarinen, a native of Finland, who emigrated in 1923 and established his influential school of art and design, the Cranbrook Academy of Art, in Bloomfield Hills, Michigan. This handsome complex includes several schools and the Academy, founded to

teach the design arts in integrated fashion, and many talented young people have studied here. From 1937 onward, Eliel Saarinen also practiced architecture with his son Eero Saarinin, who had a profound impact on the evolution of Modern architecture. Other influential émigrés included the Austrian architect Richard Joseph Neutra and Germany's Alfred Kahn, whose works are described more fully in chapter 7. Since their time, the unique panorama of North American architecture has continued to unfold, continuously reworking traditional forms and contemporary inspirations into new expressions of domestic architecture for the twenty-first century.

Above: A two-story bungalow in Jackson, California, recalls the affordable houses that became popular across the nation during the early twentieth century.

English Colonial Styles

Previous pages:
A distinctive Connecticut Valley Federal house in holiday dress, with red clapboard siding, crisp white trim, and a traditional welcoming "appleboard" above the four-paneled door.

Below: Steep thatched roofs and tiny fenced garden plots at Plimouth Plantation, Massachusetts, re-create the pioneer spirit of New England's first Puritan settlement.

The Colonial period of American architecture may be said to extend from the early 1600s, when the first of the thirteen original colonies were established or becoming consolidated, through the Revolutionary War of 1776–83. However, because there are many similarities between Georgian and Federal-style architecture (which predated the Revolution by at least a decade), the Federal period (1760–1830) is included here, comprising both the massive Jeffersonian Classical and the lighter, more decorative, Adam and Regency styles of the early 1800s.

Very few of the cottage-style and postmedieval houses of the 1600s have survived, with rare exceptions including the John Whipple House, built in 1640 in Ipswich, Massachusetts, with its second-story overhang, diamond-paned casement windows, and multiple gables. The thatched-roof dwellings of the original Puritan settlers have been re-created at the Plimouth Plantation, in Plymouth, Massachusetts, to give contemporary Americans a sense of how our forebears

lived at that time. Since reeds suitable for thatching were less available than they had been in England, many colonists in both New England and Virginia turned to hand-split cedar shingles for roofing. Cedar was valued for its durability and resistance to water damage, and shingled roofs soon displaced most of the original thatched roofs in the early colonies.

The Rhode Island stone-ender, mentioned earlier, was constructed from about 1640 in the region settled by dissenters from the rigorous Puritanism of the Massachusetts Bay Colony. The substantial cottages built here consisted of oak-plank siding nailed to the timber frame, with the north end of the house consisting almost entirely of a huge stone chimney serving the large ground-floor fireplace used for cooking, heat, and light. The fireplace had a hearth of tamped earth, and the hall, or common room, was floored with oak boards enclosed by the sill, which was set upon a fieldstone foundation. Windows were few and small to conserve heat, cut from imported English blown glass and set into lead-framed casements.

By 1690 the stone-ender was being enlarged by a lean-to kitchen addition at the back, and the medieval-style chimney might have three flues for additional fireplaces. Often a cellar was dug below the house for storage, accessed by outside doors, and a corner stairway led from the porch or front entry to the bedroom beside the chimney. Insulation was improved by more effective use of wattle-and-daub infill (woven sticks and a binding material like mud or clay) between larger structural members spaced more widely along the walls. Unlike other early houses, with chimneys of mud or clay and sticks, the stone-ender rarely burned down.

The saltbox style that evolved from the stone-ender in the late 1600s lent itself to a variety of additions as families grew and became more prosperous. The original lean-to addition at the back was often expanded to form the double-shed salt-box, and the gable-end chimney became a large central chimney with several flues. The façade was rectangular, with a centrally placed doorway flanked by two windows and a row of three windows above. On Nantucket Island, Massachusetts, where whaling was the principal occupation, the so-called Nantucket whale house was built as a single-story shingled cottage with partial lean-to additions on either side of the main house. The much larger "outshot" house was formed by adding a cluster of single-story lean-tos at the rear of a two-story saltbox. The largest of them had their own gabled roofs with a central chimney, forming an L-shaped plan with the main house.

The transition from the early colonial dwellings to the Georgian style imported from England took place with the New England farmhouse, which was first built during the late 1600s. This house ranged from one-and-one-half stories high to two-and-one-half stories (called the New England large), but the basic design was recognizable throughout the long period in which it was built (to about 1850). This farmhouse, with regional variations, would reappear from the Midwest to the far Northwest during the nineteenth century.

Its main features included a symmetrical rectangular façade with a peaked roof and a massive central chimney serving several fireplaces. Window size increased with the availability of glass, and double-hung sash windows had become the norm by 1740, usually glazed with six panes above and six below. Most houses had at least a partial cellar for the storage of root crops and tools, and the first floor

Above: An old shingled saltbox with triple shed-roofed dormer sags into ruin on Prince Edward Island. New England and Atlantic Canada share many architectural features because of their proximity and the frequent migration between the two regions.

Above: A modest frame fishing shack in Maine, raised on masonry supports, shows its colonial antecedents in everything but the metal stovepipe attached to the gable end— a nineteenth-century innovation widely used for folk and temporary housing.

retained the hall-and-parlor plan, with the hall used for cooking and the parlor as a common room. The two-story house allowed for additional headroom in the upstairs bedrooms, and more emphasis was placed on the entryway, which became more decorative as modest pilasters and pediments in the English Renaissance style were added.

By this time, twelve major English colonies were flourishing along the Atlantic Seaboard, and many of their residents had become wealthy through trade, commerce, and agriculture. They looked to London for exemplars of architecture, fashion, art, literature, and education. London, in turn, was deeply influenced by Italian Renaissance design, which set the standard for the Western world. When the English capital was nearly destroyed by fire in 1666, the way was open to modernization of medieval styles on a large scale. During the monarchies of Kings George I, II, III, and IV

(1714–1830), the Italian Renaissance influence was embraced and embodied in the style known as Georgian. This style appeared first in the Southern and mid-Atlantic colonies, since it used masonry— usually brick or stone—for construction. Some time elapsed before the Georgian style was translated into a grammar suitable for wooden buildings, so it came relatively late to New England. The most elaborate examples of the style, like the great Governor's Palace in Williamsburg, Virginia (1720), and many Southern estate houses and mansions, are illustrated in chapter 4. Here, we are concerned with substantial masonry and wooden houses built by successful businessmen, sea captains, government officials, and others from Eastern Canada to the southernmost English colonies.

As mentioned earlier, features of the Georgian style include a well-balanced symmetrical exterior, large paired chimneys at either end of the building, and an increasingly ornate entrance crowned by a pediment or by an arch. Small entry porches with pilasters might have a balustrade above, and in some cases the entire roofline carried an ornamental balustrade. Roofs might be hipped or gabled, depending upon location. The hipped roof gained favor in the South, where it was often inset with pedimented dormers of triangular or semicircular form. Almost every example, whether in wood, brick, or stone, had a Classical cornice line below the eaves.

The Georgian interior provided a degree of comfort and privacy that had been rare in early colonial houses. There were separate rooms for cooking, dining, entertaining, and sleeping, often on two floors with attic space under the roof that was sometimes utilized as servants' quarters. A triple Palladian window above the entrance often illuminated the upper hallway and added elegance to the façade. As Lester Walker points out in *American Shelter*, "By the middle of the eighteenth century, England's enthusiasm for the Italian-based Renaissance and classical forms had become almost fanatic. Manuals and journals showing works by the great Italian architect Palladio, and his English disciple, Inigo Jones, proliferated. The American colonies were experiencing a building boom, and these Renaissance books were greatly influential." In British Canada, the style was, if anything, more popular and longer-lived than it would be in the future United States.

Despite regional variations, Georgian houses retain their affinity with the tenets of Classical design in comprising three zones: a short base, forming the visual foundation; a longer central zone with balanced elements; and a shorter top story that reprises the decorative features

Below: This venerable hip-roofed masonry house on the Hudson River, in Newburgh, New York, served for a time as George Washington's headquarters in the Revolutionary War.

Below: A brick-lined New England fireplace dating from 1730, fronted by cobblestones, still sheds its warmth in the cellar of a Georgian colonial house with the characteristic central chimney.

of the other two levels. The Federal style that began to evolve about 1760 shared these features, while introducing more flexible floor plans and a more restrained type of ornamentation.

Patriots like the fiery Thomas Paine, who advocated a radical break with the Mother Country, espoused the Federal style, and colonist Benjamin Asher published the first architectural journal independent of British models: *The Country Builders Assistant: Containing a Collection of New Designs of Carpentry and Architecture* (1796). It contained full plans for designing and building the Federal-style house. Closets, small storage areas, even indoor

privies began to appear, and much of the Georgian-style embellishment was simplified or eliminated. Salem, Massachusetts, architect Samuel McIntire did pioneering work in this mode, including the Pierce-Nichols (1790) and Gardner Pingree Houses (1804), both in his native city. Other examples have been preserved in Historic Deerfield, Massachusetts, side by side with earlier New England houses as described previously. Founded in 1669, Historic Deerfield is a microcosm of architectural development in the Connecticut Valley through the late nineteenth century.

Jeffersonian Classicism originated in Virginia about 1770 and remained most influential in the South. Based on the Roman orders, which Thomas Jefferson had studied during his European travels as American minister to France in the late 1780s, it was usually built of red brick with a wooden portico painted white and flanking wings on either side of the central façade. The wings were often single-story elements, with Classical cornices that echoed the small triangular pediment over the entrance and the larger pediment supported by the portico. His model for Richmond's Virginia State Capitol building (1786) was the Augustan temple known as the Maison Carrée (16 BC) in Nimes, France, and he designed several handsome estate houses that were influenced by the late Georgian style, including Barboursville, Virginia (1817). Here, heavy wooden columns painted white gave an air of solidity to the façade, and four tall chimneys sprouted from the hipped roof. The roof was constructed so that a dome could be added over the drawing room, but this plan was never carried out. Designed for Governor James Barbour, the house had two stories, with a study, sitting room, and bedroom on the first floor along with the usual dining and drawing rooms. The kitchen was relegated to a separate outbuilding. Jefferson's life-long improvements to Monticello, his own plantation house, were influenced by designs for the Italian villa that he found in his studies of Palladio.

The Scottish-born Adam brothers, Robert, James, and William, had the largest architectural practice in England during the late 1700s, based on firsthand observation of Classical ruins in Italy and Dalmatia. The Neoclassical style they created was first used in the United States to decorate the dining-room ceiling at George Washington's Mount Vernon with what Robert Adam described as "a beautiful variety of light mouldings, gracefully formed, delicately enriched and arranged with propriety and skill."

The Harvard-educated architect Charles Bulfinch, a friend of Thomas Jefferson's, advocated the Adam style and adapted it to his own practice, which included the design of Boston's Beacon Hill. Adam-style houses were built primarily on the Eastern Seaboard for wealthy clients. Examples include the Nickels-Sortwell House in Wiscasset, Maine (1812), and the ornate Nicholas Ware House in Augusta, Georgia (1818). The latter has the twin curving stairways with wrought-iron railings leading up to the entrance that would become a popular feature of Southern townhouses and plantations.

The Regency, last of the Georgian styles to emerge in England, at the turn of the nineteenth century, was influential in the new United States primarily as a transition between the Adam style and the immensely popular Greek Revival. Its principal English exponent was architect

John Soane, who used both Greek and Roman elements to design Neoclassical houses with flat or hipped roofs and prominent doorways or porticoes, ornamented in the style that would be adopted by eclectic Beaux-Arts architects much later in the century. During the early 1800s, Soane had a strong influence on American architect William Jay, who built a number of remarkable Neoclassical townhouses in Savannah, Georgia. Modest versions of his elegant Hull-Barrow and Telfaire Houses would appear across the South as far west as the Mississippi River.

Above: This clapboard farmhouse in Weston, Vermont, with its steep gabled roof and a louver to ventilate the attic, has been modified by the addition of a modest porch with graceful columns.

11111111111111111111111111111111111

Keynote: Simplicity

The symmetrical saltbox-style Medford Farmhouse above, in East Hampton, New York, was built in 1660 with timber framing clad in shingles and weatherboard. The massive central chimney served several fireplaces. On the opposite page is Mission House in Stockbridge, Massachusetts, an early Georgian with minimal adornment—the paneled doorway, with its fluted pilasters and broken scroll pediment.

Pre-Revolutionary Homes Near Boston *Overleaf*

The historic Job Lane House in Bedford, Massachusetts (page 34), features the plain vertical-board door with unlighted transom above, which is typical of early New England's postmedieval-style dwellings. On page 35, in nearby Woburn, is the birthplace of Benjamin Thompson (1753–1814), known by his title of Count Rumford. A Loyalist who left the colonies for England in 1776, Thompson became a well-known scientist and was made a count of the Holy Roman Empire for his services to the prince of Bavaria. Later, he endowed the Rumford chair of science at Harvard University.

Island Outposts

Above, the Choate House (c. 1725), banked into a hill-side overlooking the Atlantic on Hog Island, also known as Choate Island, near Ipswich, Massachusetts. The Choate family made their home on the scenic island for some 300 years. At left, New England cottage-style shelters translated into a Western idiom on California's tranquil Mosquito Lake.

Northerly Climes *Overleaf*

A brightly trimmed clapboard cottage on Fogo Island, Newfoundland (page 38), its door propped shut by a long pole as in colonial days. On page 39, seaside style and color at a well-kept vintage home in Hart's Cove, Newfoundland, a province developed mainly by British settlers from the early 1800s.

Early America, Inside and Out

The classic center-hall Georgian house above—Wilton, in
Richmond, Virginia—shows the Southern preference for
brick construction, hipped roofs, tall chimneys, and white-
paneled wood detailing around the front door and along
the cornice line. On the opposite page is the handsome
sunroom at Chipstone, in Fox Point, Wisconsin, furnished
entirely in seventeenth- and eighteenth-century antiques
made in New England and Pennsylvania. The corner
shelves contain rare examples of period English Delftware.

Masonry Construction, New Brunswick

The landmark Keillor House in Dorchester (at left, detail above) incorporates both cut and rough stone in a classically symmetrical façade flanked by set-back wings. The double-hung sash windows, in simple surrounds, are of the familiar six-over-six-light type. Brightly painted doors—this one of vertical boards with wrought-iron hardware—are an attractive feature of the Atlantic Canadian vernacular.

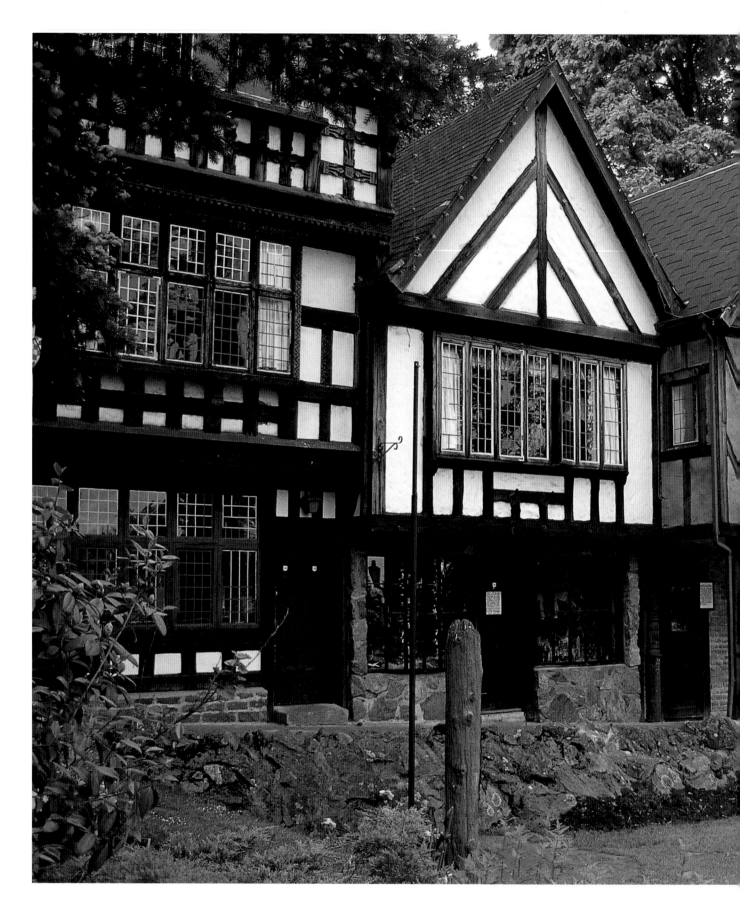

Medieval Effects

The very British city of Victoria, British Columbia, displays its heritage proudly in the half-timbered replica of Anne Hathaway's thatched cottage and traditional garden, above, and the timber-and-stucco façade of the Olde England Inn (opposite), with its second-story overhang, or jetty, and leaded-glass casement windows.

Colonial Revival Styles

The carefully tended house below, in Virginville, Pennsylvania, is representative of the Colonial Revival style that became popular nationwide from the late nineteenth century well into the twentieth. Note the quoin-like decoration at the corners and the paneled shutters flanking small-paned windows. On the opposite page is Brooks Farm, in Troy, Michigan, modeled on the masonry farmhouse of the mid-Atlantic region. The original portion of the building has a broken-pediment modillion gable and an off-center entryway framed by a portico with balustrade. It now houses the Kresge Foundation.

Craftsmanship of Rare Quality

The well-preserved kitchen above has a cavernous brick-lined fireplace framed in timber and period furnishings including the painted rocking chair in the foreground, made in New England about 1800. The pewter flagon on the mantel is the work of metalsmith Oliver Trask (1792–1847) of Beverly, Massachusetts. At right is a sturdy Pennsylvania fieldstone house that was expanded over the years. Note the break in the roofline and the separate columned entryway.

Town and Country *Overleaf*

Philadelphia's Elfreth's Alley (page 50), where some of the nation's best Federal-style townhouses may still be seen. A classical brick townhouse on Baltimore's Federal Hill (page 51), with a finely detailed entrance surmounted by a rounded toplight and framed by a brick arch. On page 52, the Gordon Trumbull House (1840), in Stonington, Connecticut, and on page 53, multilevel rooflines, embellished over the years, in Plymouth, Massachusetts.

European Influences

Previous pages: French and New England influences mingle in the coastal town of Percé, Quebec, named for the great rock formation that juts from the Gulf of St. Lawrence off the Gaspé Peninsula.

Below: Montreal's historic Chateau Ramezay, a Quebec-style masonry townhouse dating back to 1705.

While colonists from England were establishing themselves in the New World, Europeans were founding enclaves from present-day Quebec to St. Augustine, Florida; the Hudson River Valley; the Delaware Valley; and parts of the present-day Southwest, from New Mexico and Texas through the California coast. Their influence is still apparent in their initial culture areas, whether in the form of original structures (sometimes very rare, after three or four hundred years), revival styles, restorations, or translations into a contemporary idiom that is still recognizably "Southwestern," "Creole," or "Pennsylvania Dutch" (actually German), as the case may be.

As the continent became more widely inhabited by non-Native Americans, and transportation reached deep inland in the form of riverboats, canal boats, bridges, roads, and eventually, railroads, house-building ideas from many ethnic groups were combined to form the regional vernacular styles described more fully in chapter 5. Here we illustrate a broad spectrum of residential building styles indigenous to Europe and adapted to the climate, topography, available materials, and the changing technology in North America from the sixteenth through the late nineteenth centuries.

When Dutch settlers first came to the Hudson River Valley, they built small one-room cottages two stories high, with coursed fieldstone below and cedar-board cladding on the second floor, which had a steep roofline to provide some headroom.

Tiny square windows, few in number, helped to conserve heat, and a single chimney at the gable end served the stone fireplace. The largest Dutch settlement was New Amsterdam (later New York City), which saw the construction of early townhouses by 1650. As in other Hudson River Valley towns like Albany and Schenectady, these houses faced the street, presenting a brick façade that conformed to fire laws, while the other three side walls retained their wooden cladding. Architectural details were imported from Holland and Flanders, including segmental brick arches over single or paired windows and stepped gables that concealed the roofline and made the house look taller. Batten doors (made of vertical boards) were the norm, and many were in the traditional two-part Dutch style that allowed for opening the top half for ventilation and light when weather permitted. The danger posed by chimney fires, especially in close urban quarters, was decreased in the late 1600s by the introduction of ceramic-tiled roofs. Shutters were often added for insulation.

The Dutch farmhouse began as a countrified version of these townhouses, or as the long house/barn traditional in the homeland. However, the influence of neighboring colonists from England, France, and Flanders modified these buildings into a truly indigenous Dutch Colonial style between about 1680 and 1710. The straight-edged gable roof replaced the urban stepped gable in the northern part of the Valley, and readily available materials were used to build brick-walled houses on fieldstone foundations, with the bricks bound to the timber framing by pointed anchor irons. The townhouse-style front entrance was

moved to the side of the building, and chimneys appeared at both gable ends.

The overhanging Flemish eave was adopted widely in the lower Hudson River Valley, with the gable roof projecting over both front and rear walls to divert rain water from the foundation and protect entrances. Alternatively, shorter "pentroofs" projected above the entrances to both houses and barns to keep them free of rain and snow. The gambrel roof, with its double slope on each side of the ridgepole, was adopted from the English to provide more usable space on the upper level.

By 1720 much larger versions of the early fieldstone-and-cedar cottage had appeared on Long Island and Staten Island, often with central chimneys in the

Above: A dragonlike gargoyle on a New York City townhouse, modeled on the ornamental rainspouts used in Europe since the Middle Ages to protect stone and brick walls from water damage.

Above: A Chalet-style building in the town of Helena, Georgia, founded by settlers from Switzerland, the Austrian Tyrol, and the Alpine region of Germany.

gambrel roof and attic rooms for sleeping accessed by a ladder from the ground floor. In New Jersey, the flared-eave Flemish farmhouse became popular, with posts supporting the extended roofline at front and rear to form porches, or verandahs, like those adopted from the West Indies for Southern homes. The addition of paired or triple attic dormers improved space and light in the bedroom area.

The earliest permanent buildings in New France were based on the late-medieval style of northern France and centered in and around Quebec. Squared timbers were inserted into a timber sill, and the walls were infilled, or nogged, with a mixture of mud and stone covered by stucco. These early houses were usually single-story buildings with several narrow window and door openings flanked by shutters. Steeply pitched roofs were designed, like French thatched roofs, to shed rain and snow, which abounded in the frigid winters of Eastern Canada. Many farmsteads were built in

the U-shaped or enclosed-courtyard styles of Brittany and Normandy, with houses, barns, and outbuildings grouped tightly together, or sharing a common roof, for protection against the weather.

As French settlement extended outward from Quebec, all-wood construction became more prevalent; short squared timbers were slotted into place between upright studs to form walls that were covered with horizontal planks. Mud or other insulating material was used between the inner and outer walls, and openings remained few, but became more evenly spaced. Lighter timber roof frames—later, hipped roofs—became the norm, sometimes with flaring, or bellcast, eaves.

During the eighteenth century, the townhouse of Quebec and Montreal assumed a distinctive form. It was built of fieldstone, up to four stories high, and had multipaned casement windows trimmed in smooth cut stone. High end walls on the steep gable roofs acted as firebreaks, mandated to prevent the rapid spread of fire from house to house. Many handsome examples of this style may still be seen in Eastern Canada, which has also preserved the French Colonial country house, or *maison traditionelle*, with its long, low silhouette crowned by a hipped roof with flaring eaves and dormers. Variations on these styles would dominate the architecture of the Midland region, comprising the original Illinois Country and the vast Louisiana Territory of the Mississippi Valley, into the early nineteenth century, as described more fully in chapters 3 and 5.

Although the Spanish came early to the region discovered by Ponce de Leon, and named "Florida" for its luxuriant tropical vegetation, their initial settlement at St.

Augustine (1565) was little more than a naval post for the renowned Spanish treasure fleet. Surrounded by palisades, its first shelters were single-room palmetto-frond huts like those of the native Seminole, with whom there were frequent clashes. Later, simple board cottages with thatched roofs, and smokeholes rather than chimneys, were built in the hard-pressed community, which was often attacked by European enemies of the Spanish Crown, as well as hostile natives and English colonists pushing south from Chesapeake Bay to assert their claims to the region. In fact, St. Augustine was burned to the ground at least four times, but the Spanish maintained their tenuous hold here and eventually extended their influence as far west as Pensacola, on the Gulf Coast, and the lower Carolinas.

In the Southeast, Spanish settlers developed an indigenous building material known as tabby—a kind of cement formed with oyster shells, lime, and sand—and used it with the local sedimentary rock formed of multilayered coquina shell to build more spacious and comfortable houses in the style of their homeland. They centered around the patio, which often had a stone well and various plantings, and had in-line rooms to promote the circulation of cooling breezes. Cooking was relegated to a separate building, and loggias, or open passageways, still common in Florida today, connected various parts of the house. More elaborate dwellings had balconied second stories, influenced by immigrants from both the Canary Islands and the Caribbean. Red-tiled roofs were characteristic of Spanish architecture in both the Southeast and the Southwest, especially California, where the long chain of

Spanish missions, *haciendas*, and *presidios* (forts) set the tone for regional architecture on the lower Pacific Coast.

To this day, bungalows, ranch houses, public buildings, churches, and estates bearing the imprint of Old Spain are being constructed from New England to northern California. Variously known as Mediterranean, Mission, Spanish Colonial Revival, and Pueblo Revival, they reflect the influence of native styles, both Mexican and Southwestern, on Spanish colonists, who shared similar building techniques. Adobe construction had come to Spain with the Moorish conquest from North Africa, and the terraced adobe pueblos of New Mexico struck a familiar chord. Both adobe bricks, made of sun-dried mud and straw, and puddled, or liquid, adobe, were used to build dwellings that shared several characteristics: thick masonry walls of adobe brick or rubblestone, covered with stucco or liquid adobe, and sheltered by low-pitched roofs supported on timber *vigas*, the ends of which protrude through the upper wall of the façade. Alternatively, the roof may be flat, with low parapets

Below: Rough-hewn timber supports (vigas), originally used by Pueblo peoples and Hispanic settlers, protrude from a masonry façade in Pueblo Bonito, New Mexico. Such timbers served to uphold both floor and roof beams.

Above: *Zigzag rail fencing frames a French military camp of log and fieldstone, raised on Mississippi's Natchez Trace in 1812.*

all around. Patios, colonnades, deeply set windows, and hooded fireplaces figure prominently, while the most elaborate houses and public buildings demonstrate the influence of the imposing Spanish Baroque style in a wealth of molded and carved ornamentation.

Seventeenth-century colonists from central and northern Europe first settled in the Delaware Valley and built timber-framed houses of the late-medieval German type, and Swedish log cabins, or cribs, of various styles that became identified with frontier life, as described in the following chapter. From about 1675, Germans who emigrated to the Delaware Valley, or Middle Colonies, built small farmhouses of fieldstone on timber framing, much of which was left exposed in the style we call half-timbering. These dwellings were entered through the kitchen, whose fireplace also heated the

adjacent common room. Gabled roofs were supported with complex timber frameworks, as in the Rhineland.

As families increased in size and affluence, they often added a second story and began to ornament their interiors with richly carved woodwork and painting. The original half-timbered exterior, called *Fachwerk*, was often modified to form a ground floor of fieldstone with a second floor of notched logs. Massive stone chimneys served the fireplaces.

When Amish settlers came to eastern Pennsylvania in the early eighteenth century, having been driven from both Switzerland and Germany for their separatist Mennonite faith, they built in the style that soon became known as "Pennsylvania Dutch" (because the word for German, *Deutsch*, was misunderstood). Both German and Swiss techniques were used to build substantial stone houses, and barns on timber frameworks that were often "banked" into a hillside to provide warmth in winter and summer coolness. Eventually, "Pennsylvania" barns, houses, and outbuildings were adopted in New England, Eastern Canada (which also welcomed Mennonite immigrants), and the Midwest, including Ohio and Indiana. Fortunately, many descendants of these settlers have maintained their original homesteads as working farms, adding to them over the years to form close-knit ethnic communities. German-Americans built two-story masonry townhouses in cities including Philadelphia and their buildings also rose in Maryland, Virginia, and North Carolina. They are so well constructed that many examples have survived in the form of houses, grist mills, and historic inns.

During the nineteenth century, wars, persecution, and poverty in many parts of Europe brought a new and diverse wave of immigrants to the United States and Canada. In the time-honored way of immigrants everywhere, they worked hard and saved all they could to bring additional members of their families to the New World, which offered many opportunities, including the acquisition of cheap land, to those with the hardihood to take advantage of them. A microcosm of such ethnic settlements sprang up along Wisconsin's Lake Michigan shoreline, where no fewer than thirty communities were founded, ranging from Austrian, Belgian, and Czech to Icelandic, Irish, and Polish. Their influence on North American residential architecture is described and illustrated in chapters 3 and 5.

Below: An Old World German farmstead in the half-timbered style, with a threshing floor between the house (at left) and connected barn, reconstructed at the Museum of Frontier Culture in Staunton, Virginia.

San Diego: Old Town

California's Spanish heritage is apparent in these pho-
tographs from San Diego's Old Town Historic District,
which includes the whitewashed adobe house above,
with its geometric stepped entryway and red-tiled roof,
and the long, low Casa de Estudillo (right), which
escaped the devastating fire that swept through the district in 1872 and has since been faithfully restored.

Spanish-Moorish Influences

These examples from the East and West Coasts show styles influenced by the Moorish occupation of Spain from the early 700s. The Pasadena, California, house above resembles those of the mountainous province of Andalusia, southern Spain (controlled by the Moors until 1492), in its severe façade and wrought-iron grille-work at ground-floor window and balcony. The New York City townhouse on the opposite page has a curving gated entrance stairway with colorful ceramic tiles hand-decorated in geometric patterns like those seen in medieval Spanish mosques and public buildings as well as in the Islamic Middle East.

Delaware Valley Masonry

The Mid-Atlantic states have many old buildings in the tradition of sturdy Germanic stonework. On the opposite page is a historic shelter on the Potomac Canal in Washington, D.C., with a high gable wall, almost windowless, that rises to a massive chimney. Below, Worcester, Pennsylvania's, Peter Wentz farmstead, built in 1758, shows how irregular fieldstones, with their flat sides facing outward, were cemented together to form weathertight walls. During the Revolutionary War, George Washington used the farmhouse to plan the Battle of Germantown.

Pennsylvania Dutch Country

Eastern Pennsylvania's Lancaster County was originally settled by many German immigrants, including the Mennonite builder of the Hans Herr House, below, which was built in 1719 of uncoursed sandstone. It is the oldest Mennonite meeting place in North America and the oldest building in Lancaster County. Members of this sect worship in their homes, taking turns in hosting the congregation. Operated as a museum, the property is one of the best-preserved examples of medieval Germanic architecture in the Untied States.

French-Canadian Structures

Flaring eaves, triple dormers, and a second-level entry porch with slender supports infer the French antecedents of the modest country house opposite, in Rosemere, Quebec. Many such cottages were constructed in the Mississippi Valley, where the French claimed sovereignty as far south as New Orleans.

Overleaf: A faithful replica of the French-style stockade on Lake Superior, at Grand Portage National Monument, Minnesota—once a major fur-trading center for Canadian *voyageurs* and the native Ojibwa.

Quebec-style Townhouse

The Pierre du Calvet House (1725), in Montreal's Old City (opposite; detail below), has typical rough-cut field-stone walls bonded by mortar and the high end walls required by local law as firebreaks after a major fire in 1721. Built by a Huguenot merchant, this *maison de ville* has the hand-forged S-shaped bars that helped solidify the structure against shifts caused by expansion and contraction in freezing and thawing conditions.

Louisiana Country Houses

Acadian traditions dating back to 1755, when French residents of Quebec and the Canadian coast were expelled by the British, are apparent in these planters' homes on the lower Mississippi River. The hip-roofed example above—Louisiana's Destrehan Plantation—was built in the French Colonial style in 1787, enlarged in 1810, and partially converted to the Greek Revival style before the Civil War. The double galleries are now supported by Doric columns. On the opposite page is Shadows-on-the-Teche, built during the 1830s on the south bank of the Bayou Teche in New Iberia by David Weeks, a sugar-cane grower. Four generations of the Weeks family made their home here until 1958, when the property became a National Trust historic site.

French Quarter, New Orleans

Perhaps the most European of all U.S. cities, New Orleans has preserved its French and Creole heritage in the eight-by-five-block *Vieux Carré*, known in English as the French Quarter, laid out in 1721 as a planned city and now a preserved district that attracts tourists from around the world. Its handsome brick and stone buildings, many encircled by elaborate wrought-iron balconies, as seen in the detail above and on Dumaine Street (opposite), add to the historic district's charm. Most of the structures here postdate the great fire that swept through the port city in 1794.

Campobello Island

New Brunswick's proximity to the Maine border gives this coastal province on the Bay of Fundy an international character, as seen on historic Campobello Island, which lies just off Maine's (and the United States') easternmost mainland point. The Franklin D. Roosevelt family chose this scenic, peaceful location for their rambling summer house, shown on the opposite page, with its multiple shed dormers and shuttered windows. Below is the spacious Hubbard House, which has a graceful flared roofline with front-facing gable and attractive multipaned windows. Both houses have elements reminiscent of traditional European building styles — respectively, Dutch and French — and affinities with New England Colonial architecture.

Frontier and Folk Housing

Right: *Heritage Village, in Green Bay, Wisconsin, gives us a glimpse of the nineteenth-century buildings put up by the multiethnic immigrants who settled along the Lake Michigan shoreline. The state's Ethnic Settlement Trail traces the new communities formed by almost fifty nationalities.*

Previous pages:
A Revolutionary-era community, including a working farm, restored at Pennsylvania's Bedford Historic Village. A contemporary English traveler (1770) observed: "Almost all the houses hereabouts were built either of stone or bricks, but those of stone were more numerous." Substantial two-story log houses have also been moved here from other parts of Bedford County.

A host of shelters that had no pretensions to grandeur became part of North America's built landscape between the mid-1600s and the early twentieth century. They range from the familiar log cabin imported by Swedish and German settlers of the original thirteen colonies to the slave quarters of Southern plantations, nineteenth-century miners' shanties, railroad-tie shacks put up by laborers on the ever-widening rail network, and crude homesteads built on the frontier from Appalachia to the West Coast. Also covered here are the simple communal dwellings of Utopian communities including the Shakers, the Owenites, the German founders of Iowa's Amana communities, and other religious and spiritual fellowships like those of the early Mormons, who did extensive missionary work in Europe. Their immigrant converts brought several new ethnic building styles to their new communities in the Midwest, Southwest, and Salt Lake City, Utah, their principal foundation.

The original single-room log cabin, chinked with mud, moss, or clay, was often enlarged within a generation and took on new forms as it spread from the Delaware Valley along the Ohio River and south into what it is now Kentucky and neighboring states. The so-called saddlebag house (two rooms served by a central chimney) resembles the Swedish cell-type cottage, which was often roofed with turf. A similar plan was that of the Fenno-Scandinavian gatehouse—two log cribs roofed by a single span covering a central wagonway. In the United States, this design came to be known as the dogtrot cabin, which was instrumental in the evolution of the ranch house.

Many North German and Scandinavian log houses had a separate front door to each of the two rooms and a shed-roofed porch. Domestic animals were often housed in one of the two cribs of a dogtrot-style cabin; in other cases, a separate log barn was built, and outbuildings were added as needed for storage of tools, seeds, and other necessities. The breezeway between the two cabins was sometimes called a possumtrot by pioneers in the southern Appalachians, who hunted possums, squirrels, and rabbits for food.

Several types of notching were used to join log cabins at the corners, ranging from simple axe-hewn depressions to the more complex vee-shaped and half-dovetail styles. Swedish settlers removed the bark from their logs to prevent decay. Plank door and window jambs framed the openings, and their seventeenth-century fieldstone fireplaces had chimneys of mud-lined sticks. The walls needed no framing, and the roof was supported by a central ridge log on "king posts," flanked by shorter "queen posts" holding a purlin log — a lower support for the rafters descending from the ridgepole. The rafters were made of split logs and covered by split-cedar shingles. It was an economical, quickly constructed shelter, with a floor of tamped earth (later planks) and small openings to conserve heat. In warmer climates, the windows were larger and more numerous.

Log homes took on new configurations as the frontier expanded westward. By 1780 pioneers in Kentucky were building simple cabins with squared logs and vee-notched corners. A fieldstone fireplace protruded from one end wall, with a square chimney of wattle and daub — thin branches covered with mud — like that of the Swedish prototypes.

During the early nineteenth century, Southern plantation owners often built one-room slave cabins with walls of log and brick fireplaces and chimneys at the gable end opposite the door. The "mossback" log cabin was built by Midwestern lumberjacks in the Great Lakes states from about 1840. It was heated by a wood-burning stove rather than a fireplace, and the roof logs were shaped like large tiles to shed rainwater. A metal chimney strapped to an end wall served the stove. Similar tin chimneys identified the single-room log cabin of the mining frontier, built of notched round logs and roofed with overlapping boards caulked with moss and hay. Some Western settlers added an enclosed porch by extending the log walls while leaving the gable end of the roof open below the ridgepole. A low log railing flanked the porch entry, leaving one end of the house open to the outdoors. In some areas, short lengths of stovewood set in concrete mortar, inset with door and window frames, formed the walls. Second- and third-generation cabins were often built with durable concrete chinking between the logs.

As the geographic center of the United States, Indiana, with its southern border along the Kentucky state line, has examples of many architectural styles, including those of the trans-Appalachian "first frontier." The Lincoln Pioneer Village, in Rockport, consists of eighteen cabins, from dwellings to a buggy shed, church, and

Below: Slave-quarter cabins with gabled roofs extended to form deep front porches were built at Louisiana's Magnolia Plantation to house the families whose arduous labor cultivated the sugar cane.

general store. Eventually, some log houses would comprise two or three stories over an excavated cellar. Scots-Irish immigrants and restless Americans moving on, side by side with a new wave of German and Scandinavian settlers, would make this form of housing prevalent throughout the Midwest and beyond. In Wisconsin there is a preserved Cornish miners' colony, Pendarvis, at Mineral Point and an agricultural village at Stonefield, along with the historic palisaded fort on Madeline Island, which recalls the exploration and settlement of the Apostle Islands.

A hybrid style of folk house popular in the South is the "shotgun house," so called because a shot fired through the front door would pass straight through to the back yard. It originated in central Africa and came to New Orleans by way of Haitians from the West Indies in the early nineteenth century. These houses are usually one room wide and several rooms deep, their narrow façades defined by a modest front porch—another feature that

originated in African architecture and became typical of the American house. It was devised to provide relief from tropical heat and humidity, and adopted widely in the Southeast, where it was introduced by slaves in a thatched-roof form and continued by freedmen after the Civil War— tenant farmers, laborers, and others. The thatched roof did not disappear from African-American farm outbuildings until well into the twentieth century.

The Great Plains—which early explorers had described as "the Great American Desert"—proved to have extremely fertile soil, but early settlers were hard pressed to build shelters equal to the region's climatic extremes—long, cold winters and very hot summers. Timber was scarce, and potential building stone was covered by deep layers of sod bound by thick roots of prairie grass. Pioneers in Kansas, Nebraska, the Dakotas, and surrounding regions often built dugout shelters roofed and walled with thick bricks of sod carved from the land, or sod

Right: Solid Shaker masonry in the simple New England Colonial style forms a serene façade at Mount Lebanon, New York, which preserves the memory of this dedicated sect sprung from the peace-loving Quakers.

houses on timber framing. The invention of the steel plow made it possible to cut through the topsoil to build shelter and grow crops, and the original sod houses and barns were often extended by shed-like additions made of precut boards, as sawmills became more widespread. Brick was used mainly near transport centers served by rail or waterways.

Settlement came even later to the Canadian prairie provinces of Manitoba, Saskatchewan, and Alberta, where many Ukrainian immigrants arrived in the late 1800s. Their shelters were built of log or stone, with gabled or hipped roofs, sited for southern exposure. The earliest examples had hipped-and-gabled roofs covered with thatch, like those on the European steppe. The exteriors were whitewashed with lime, and interior walls were insulated with mud and straw. Eventually, log houses across North America would be clad in weatherboards, obscuring their original form of construction.

Building styles in the arid Southwest were an amalgam of Native American and imported masonry techniques, differing mainly in their roof treatments. Spanish Colonial houses of the pitched-roof type sometimes used shingled roofs over timber framing; more often, they had low-pitched roofs covered with Spanish tile—half-cylinders of red clay. The flat-roofed adobe house had heavy horizontal timbers (called *vigas*) embedded in the masonry walls to support the heavy roof of earth or mortar, which was drained by cylindrical rainspouts to prevent collapse. In southern California, shedlike roofs with overhanging eaves were covered with tar—a roofing material that became widespread with the availability of factory-made tarpaper. Some of the early colonial roofs were thatch-covered, but most surviving examples have been reroofed with either shingles or metal.

Several decades before the Mexican War of 1846–48 brought vast areas of former Hispanic territory under U.S. sovereignty, Anglo immigrants were bringing their own modifications to Southwestern architecture. These included double-hung

Above: A second-generation log cabin from Tennessee features prominent drains from the gutter under the eaves to funnel rainwater through leaf screens for storage in rain barrels.

sash windows and the addition of framed shingled roofs to flat-roofed masonry houses. In southern California, the Monterey style evolved with the addition of a second story extended by a cantilevered porch. New Mexico, western Texas, and Arizona developed Territorial styles including the use of brick, rather than adobe, to form the low parapet of the flat-roofed house. Shedlike additions and outbuildings were added as family

enterprises became established. The Spanish Colonial-style *hacienda* had porches in the form of colonnades that provided ventilation and passageways to various rooms and access to the traditional inner courtyard. These were substantial houses built by successful merchants, ranchers, and farmers.

The Creole cottage form was brought to the Louisiana Territory by French Canadian (Cajun) immigrants who were familiar with long-span roof-framing methods. These side-gabled houses are usually two rooms deep, with an integral porch below the extended roofline. In and around New Orleans, urban and rural Creole cottages were built at least until the Civil War. Few survive in their original forms in the *Vieux Carré*, or French Quarter, of New Orleans. The French influence remains unmistakable, but it was affected by the great fires that almost destroyed the district in 1788 and '91. The original Creole houses often had delicate wrought-iron balconies framing second-story French doors, but the extensive use of cast-iron balconies along the full façade and the sides of the building was an innovation of the late nineteenth century.

The architecture of North America's Utopian communities was in keeping with the simplicity of their lifestyle, work ethic, and commitment to their ideals. The Shakers had evolved from the English Quakers, or Society of Friends, and faced similar persecution in their homeland for their renunciation of the established Church of England, with its hierarchy and ritual. Committed to celibate communal living, they built simple two-story frame houses in the New England style from the late 1700s, settling mainly in New York and Massachusetts. Named for the fervor of their liturgical dances, in which they experienced the Inner Light they sought, the Shakers strove for simplicity and perfection in their homes, crafts, and husbandry.

The Mennonites, who settled more widely across North America and formed a number of sects, were also known for their industry and honesty. Some of them built house/barns in the style of their Swiss and German homelands, while the Amish sect became best known for their banked houses and barns, partially built into hillsides for both insulation and durability. The Amish worshipped in their homes, transporting benches and prayer books from one homestead to another, and formed large extended families that shared living space and daily tasks from eastern Pennsylvania into Indiana, Ohio, and other Midwestern states. Most of their buildings are of masonry and timber construction, designed for utility rather than beauty, but with harmonious proportions, generous gardens, and large fenced enclosures for domestic animals, including the Standardbred road horses that the Old Amish still use for transportation and farm work, shunning electricity and internal-combustion engines.

Amana communities in Iowa were formed by another group of German immigrants who established seven self-supporting "colonies" centered around the village church, which was a simple frame building similar in style to the Quaker meetinghouse. The Amanites, or "Inspirationists," held and worked their land in common, raising sheep for wool and compounding herbal remedies for sale. They also built sturdy mills on local streams to grind grain, and maintained good relations with their neighbors. When

they moved away from agriculture into the production of electrical appliances in the early twentieth century, their villages became a kind of cooperative, rather than a spiritual community, but their traditional way of life may be explored in present-day Historic Amana, which has preserved many aspects of the original foundation. These and other Utopian communities, many of which are illustrated in the following pages, contributed to North American spiritual and cultural life out of all proportion to their numbers.

Below: Distinctive German timber framing securing wall insulation of bundled reeds marks this sturdy colonial shelter at Staunton, Virginia's, Museum of American Frontier Culture. Note the weathertight tile roof and the flared eave, seen at right, a style that was also used by Dutch and Flemish builders.

The Early American Dream

Rich land, majestic stands of timber, and vast mountain ranges that promised still wider vistas beyond combined to make North Americans a "westering people" who set out to stake their claims with little more than an axe for hewing wood and a rifle for hunting game. On the previous pages, a rainbow provides a stunning backdrop for a simple log cabin in Canada's sparsely populated Yukon Territory. Below, vee-notched logs were used to construct these shingle-roofed cabins for George Washington's cold and hungry army during the Revolutionary War: Valley Forge National Historic Park, Pennsylvania.

Weathertight Walls and Roofing

Nineteenth-century pioneers in Manitoba, Canada's prairie country, built this snug shelter of heavily chinked squared logs, with a massive fieldstone fireplace, plank flooring, sleeping loft, and strap-hinged door of native pine. It has been installed in Winnipeg's Museum of Man and Nature.

Native Stone

A Mormon family made its home in the tiny Behunin Cabin (above), built in 1882 at the foot of a rugged escarpment in what is now Utah's Capitol Reef National Park. Multicolored desert rubblestone and a deep window embrasure are all that remains of the Mormon-built shelter at right, which blends seamlessly with the landscape at Lee's Ferry, Arizona, near the Colorado River.

Remnants of Western Settlement
Sagging timbers support the dugout shelter (opposite) called Luna's Jacal, in Big Bend National Park, Texas, a land of dramatic cliffs and desert bisected by the Rio Grande. Peña Mountain looms in the background. Below, ruddy stonework doorways to a sun-gilded ruin at Campo Seco, Calaveras County, California.

Timber Country

At right, an abandoned log cabin in the Canadian Yukon is the vantage point for this view of the isolated ghost town of Big Salmon. Below, a giant sequoia dwarfs a log cabin screened by trees rimming Circle Meadow in California's Sequoia National Park. Early settlers in the West found seemingly inexhaustible supplies of timber in the abundant forests of present-day California, Oregon, Washington, British Columbia, the Yukon, and Alaska.

A Desert Oasis *Overleaf*

A homesteader's cabin of squared logs raised on a timber sill, with shingled roof and gables, surveys the remote vastness of Utah's Capitol Reef National Park.

Time-honored Building Materials

The dogtrot log cabin, with a breezeway between two cribs, was a versatile shelter based on Swedish prototypes. One crib was generally used as housing, the other for storage, or as a livestock shelter. The covered opening between them often served as a wagonway. Such cabins, forerunners of the later ranch style, were once a common sight throughout the South; this well-preserved example (right), built of log and fieldstone, is located in Stonewall, Texas.

The wall and door detail below, from a cabin in Fredericksburg, Texas, shows mixed building materials—fieldstone and timber—that were sometimes overlaid by weatherboard or stucco cladding and became exposed as the protective coating weathered away. The rustic timber door hangs on wrought-iron hinges that were probably hand-forged by a local blacksmith.

Frame Shelters

Above, a multilevel roofline crowned by dormer windows, sturdy brick chimneys, and a classical belfry at Canterbury Shaker Village, Massachusetts. Nestled among the towering evergreens and all but enveloped in snow, a cozy frame cabin heated by a woodstove holds its own on Mount Baker, in Washington State's beautiful Cascade range (opposite).

Grand Teton Homestead *Overleaf*
A time-worn log home, with a central brick chimney, and its outbuildings have begun to show the effects of the elements in their spectacular setting in the narrow fertile valley on the eastern side of the magnificent Grand Teton range, Wyoming.

Homes Far from Home

Above, a rickety wooden house raised on stilts to discourage insects, built near the Polodu Valley in Niulii, Hawaii, largest of the Hawaiian Islands. Mark Twain wrote of his travels here in *Roughing It* (1872): "I saw luxurious banks and thickets of flowers, fresh as a meadow after a rain, and glowing." On the previous pages, gabled and shed-roofed buildings raised by hopeful Forty-Niners together at Bodie, California, site of the nation's best-preserved gold-mining town.

Opposite, a rambling Pacific Northwestern homestead on scenic Shaw Island, in the San Juan archipelago, combined logs, weatherboard, bricks, and shingles — now giving way to the elements.

Mansions,
Estates,
and Plantations

Substantial town and country houses designed by architects or master builders found a place in the North American landscape as early as the seventeenth century. Among the earliest was the Southern cross house (c. 1650), so called for its cruciform plan. Essentially an expanded version of the medieval hall-and-parlor house, this brick manor included a passageway between the ground-floor hall and dining room. The kitchen, with slave quarters above, was moved to a separate building reached by a corridor or breezeway. Front and rear porches were added, and large dormers for the upstairs bedrooms. A still more elaborate variation on this theme was the Jacobean manor house of the mid-Atlantic coast, which had high parapet walls at either end with stepped or curvilinear gables in the Flemish style.

By 1700 the increasing number of plantations along the navigable waterways of the South had fostered the Plantation Colonial house, usually sited on a hill above a river, on which the crops were transported. According to architectural historian Lester Walker, the author of *American Shelter* (Overlook Press, 1981): "The plantation house was first developed in South Carolina by the Huguenots [French Protestant émigrés] near the end of the seventeenth century. It was unusual in that it had a main entrance on the river side as well as the plantation side. The house had no traditional front or back. The design stressed cross-ventilation by placing the rooms next to each other in single file, while providing shade for the two long walls with a piazza or roofed porch, a method of cooling borrowed from settlers from the West Indies."

These prototype plantation houses had hipped gabled roofs, full-length (French) windows for maximum light and ventilation, and long porches that would become typical of regional country houses on this scale. Among the best-known evolutions are the Georgian-style Gunston Hall (1758), George Washington's Mount Vernon (1743), and Thomas Jefferson's Monticello, which was a work in progress from 1767 until 1826. As the Greek Revival style swept across the continent after 1800, stimulated by the mansions and public buildings of the new capital at Washington, D.C., many of our most impressive plantation houses were built in this Classical style, from South Carolina and Georgia to the Mississippi Delta.

The stately homes of French Canada and colonial New England were inspired by medieval and Early Renaissance styles derived from the mother countries. In Quebec and Montreal, masonry construction was the norm, with Classical details including pediments, cut-stone quoins at the corners of the building and around door and window openings, carved brackets at the cornice line, and hooded

Below: One of the nation's best-known landmarks, Thomas Jefferson's Monticello, the Virginia plantation house that he designed and redesigned for a lifetime in his own Greco-Roman style, called Jeffersonian Classicism.

dormers ornamenting the roofline. In New England and the mid-Atlantic region, wood and brick were the favored building materials, used to impressive effect by architects including Samuel McIntire of Salem, Massachusetts; Charles Bulfinch of Boston; Benjamin H. Latrobe of Philadelphia and Virginia; and William Jay of Savannah, Georgia. As the following plates illustrate, they worked in a variety of styles, from Anglo-Palladian to Georgian, Federal, Adam, and Regency. However, it was the Greek Revival that dominated nineteenth-century architecture until the Civil War of 1861–65. According to the British historans P. Leslie Waterhouse and R.A. Cordingley, the authors of *The Story of Architecture* (B.T. Batsford, 1950):

"The Greek Revival was followed with intense fervour throughout the firmly settled parts of America, and for fifty years or so became almost a national style. Ancient precedent was not followed scrupulously, but was adapted in a free and fresh way to suit American occasions and materials. The spirit of the Greek originals was, however, admirably caught, and there was generally much less admixture of Roman and Renaissance elements in the American buildings than in those of the so-called Greek Revival in Britain and European countries."

Excellent examples of the style may be seen from Eastern Canada (where it is generally called the Neoclassical style) to the trans-Mississippi West. Greek Revival mansions are characterized by symmetrical plans, with rooms opening from a central hall; low-pitched rooflines; one- or two-story columned porticoes along the façade; a wide band of Classical trim below the eaves; and detailing including pediments, pilasters, fretwork, keyhole

Left: A handsome Octagonal villa with Italianate detailing in Hudson, Wisconsin, inspired by the mid-nineteenth-century ideas of designer Orson Squire Fowler, as outlined in his book A Home for All.

designs, and balustrades. Canada favored columns in the Ionic and Doric modes, while the Corinthian order was the most prominent in the United States.

A close competitor in popularity from the late 1830s onward was the Gothic Revival style, imported from England and popularized by architect Alexander Jackson Davis and his colleague Andrew Jackson Downing, a landscape architect and writer of rare talent and energy. Richard Upjohn was instrumental in bringing the Gothic to pre-eminence in ecclesiastical architecture, while Davis and Downing reinterpreted the medieval stone manor house for wealthy East Coast clients. Their designs conformed to the lay of the land, with asymmetrical massing that created a picturesque, rambling effect, ornamented by turrets, pinnacles, battlements, pointed arches, and other details borrowed from Gothic castles and cathedrals. Where cut stone was used, as in

Right: The fifty-two-room Lockwood-Mathews mansion (1864) in Norwalk, Connecticut, combines French, Romanesque, and Classical features in the eclectic Victorian mode. Designed by Danish-American architect Detlef Lienau, it is now a museum.

Davis's design for Lyndhurst (1840), in Tarrytown, New York, and other mansions on the lower Hudson River, the result was an elegant country house that was entirely fresh to the popular imagination and inspired a host of imitators in various styles and materials. For himself, Downing designed the English Gothic house he called Highland Gardens, at Newburgh, New York, while architects Calvert Vaux and F. Clarke Withers designed mansions including Robins Villa, Idlewild, and Tioronda. Tall, thin chimneys and steeply pitched roofs crowned by finials emphasized the vertical thrust of the building, enhanced by long, narrow diamond-paned windows and bays crowned by hand-carved stone tracery. When the house was built of wood, such tracery was known as "gingerbread," or Carpenter Gothic, executed by steam-powered scroll saws and other recently developed tools. Often, as in the case of the Greek Revival, earlier houses were reoriented, enlarged, or converted to the new perpendicular style, which spread nationwide through a host of plan and pattern books.

From about 1855, many other picturesque and eclectic styles enjoyed popularity with the newly affluent. These included the Italian-villa style—arguably the most influential of the multifaceted Victorian era. Downing recommended it in his widely read *Architecture of Country Houses*: "The irregularity in the masses of the edifice and the shape of the roof" [dominated by a square campanile, or bell tower] resulted in "the sky outline of a building in a style extremely picturesque." The floor plan was usually L- or T-shaped, the windows round-headed, sometimes grouped in pairs or threes, and the projecting eaves supported by ornately carved brackets, which led to the nickname "Hudson River Bracketed." Red ceramic tile was often used as a roofing material. Close cousins of this country-house style were the cubic Italianate, with central cupola for light and ventilation, which often had paired brackets and twin chimneys; and the urban brownstone, with stone steps to the main floor, raised above street level, and narrow three- or four-story façades with Italianate detailing.

Several other styles waxed and waned rather quickly, including the Octagon house espoused by the American designer Orson Squire Fowler, which also boasted a rooftop cupola. Its rooms fanned out from a central hall, and the exterior could be adorned in any style, including the exotic Moorish motifs employed by architect Samuel Sloane for the still-unfinished mansion/museum called Longwood, in Natchez, Mississippi, whose construction was interrupted by the Civil War. The decades around that conflict saw the French Empire style, with its distinctive mansard roofline, tall windows featuring elaborate surrounds, extensive use of wrought-iron crestwork, and strong cornices (French curbs) at the top and bottom of the roof slopes.

The Exotic Revival was variously expressed in Egyptian, Etruscan, Persian, and other Eastern styles adapted to public buildings, as well as in expensive dwellings commissioned by financiers, artists, and others who could afford to defy convention on a lavish scale. More widespread and long-lasting was the Renaissance Revival style, based on the palaces of Renaissance-era Rome and Florence, as introduced from England by the architect John Notman in 1845. Essentially Classical and academic in spirit, it comprised a three-story plan articulated by belt courses and constructed of finely cut ashlar stone with rusticated (rough-cut) quoins. The design of the window frames varied from floor to floor, and the entry was framed by an arcade, or by pilasters supporting Classic entablatures. Later, North American architects trained at the Parisian École de Beaux Arts, and such illustrated journals as *American Architect and Building News*

and *Canadian Architect and Builder*, would make the Beaux-Arts style a synonym for palatial town and country houses. One of the best-known examples is The Breakers, in Newport, Rhode Island, built by Richard Morris Hunt for Cornelius Vanderbilt II (1896).

The late nineteenth century was markedly eclectic, with expensive houses ranging from the indigenous Stick style—characterized by diagonal "stick work" that recalled half-timbering—to multi-textured High Victorian Gothic masonry houses based on examples from northern Italy. The delightful and diverse Queen Anne Revival style, introduced to the United States during the Philadelphia Centennial of 1876, was embraced with enthusiasm as the culmination of all the Victorian styles. It combined Gothic and Classical motifs including corner towers, bay and oriel windows, exterior appliqué work loosely described as "Eastlake" (to the dismay of English furniture and interior designer Charles Eastlake), pilasters,

Below: The John Bremond Jr. House in Austin, Texas, is an elegant mansard-roofed essay in the Beaux-Arts style, with an unusual double gallery articulated by slender columns.

Right: The imposing plantation house Nottaway, in White Castle, Louisiana (1859), combines Greek Revival and Italian Renaissance elements to impressive effect. Note the wide overhang of the bracketed eaves, in keeping with the scale of the building.

porches, stained glass, turned posts for balustrades, terra-cotta panels, and more. From expansive East Coast summer places to colorful San Francisco townhouses, Queen Anne reigned supreme in domestic architecture for several decades.

A distinctive indigenous style emerged in the late Romanesque Revival work of Henry Hobson Richardson, which won accolades at home and abroad. His buildings featured rusticated masonry walls, deeply set windows, massive arches, short stone piers instead of columns, and circular towers with conical "witch's cap" roofs. His Trinity Church in Boston (1872) was a landmark in American architecture, and the Richardsonian Romanesque style still resounds in numerous estate designs, railway stations, and residential works including Chicago's John Glessner House (1885).

The turn of the twentieth century saw prosperity—and architecture—rising to new heights, as exemplified by period mansions in the Norman, Chateauesque, Tudor Revival, and Georgian (or Colonial) Revival styles, the latter inspired

by the influential firm of McKim, Mead and White, who also did landmark work in the eclectic Beaux-Arts, or Renaissance Revival, style. Their masterpiece is probably the jewel-like J. Pierpont Morgan Library (1906) in New York City.

California's answer to the Colonial Revival style was the Mission style, which generated a popular Spanish Colonial Revival, which included Pueblo and Mediterranean modes, that would be built nationwide. The Mission style appealed to American proponents of the Arts and Crafts Movement, who sought a return to unpretentious vernacular designs and solid craftsmanship. It is an architectural anomaly that the reform-minded English designer William Morris and his colleagues, who repudiated shoddy machine-made objects and espoused medieval-style handcraftsmanship, ended up producing beautiful goods that only the wealthy could afford. In Europe, they influenced the elegant Art Nouveau and Aesthetic Movements, the latter of which was parodied by Gilbert and Sullivan in their popular 1881 operetta *Patience:*

*Though the Philistines may jostle, you will
rank as an apostle in the high aesthetic band,
If you walk down Picadilly with a poppy or
a lily in your medieval hand.*

In the United States, Louis Sullivan and
his pupil Frank Lloyd Wright would lead
the Arts and Crafts Movement in new
directions, as seen in chapter 7. Wright's
horizontal, broad-eaved Prairie Houses,
built for wealthy clients in suburban
Chicago including Ward Willets and
Frederick H. Robie, broke new ground
with open, cross-axial plans that pin-
wheeled out from a central core to estab-
lish an organic relationship between
house and site. His mature style reached
its culmination in the landmark house
designed for Edgar Kaufmann at Bear
Run, Pennsylvania, in 1935: Fallingwater.

Classicism and the various picturesque
and revival styles would continue to
dominate American architecture until
the 1930s, when the International style
came to fore, as described in chapter 7.
Influential Eclectic designers of the early
twentieth century included Bernard
Maybeck, architect of the Hopps House
(1906) in Moss Valley, California; Julia
Morgan, who designed part of the vast
complex commissioned by William
Randolph Hearst at San Simeon,
California (1917–47); Frank Furness, who
carried out more than 600 commissions
in the Philadelphia area; George Browne
Post, who won the American Institute of
Architects Gold Medal in 1911; and
Richard Morris Hunt's sons, Richard H.
and Joseph H. Hunt, who became prominent architects in their own right.

***Left:** Longwood, in
Natchez, Mississippi, is
a unique High Victorian
Octagonal house with
exotic features including
the bulb-shaped dome
on the rooftop belvedere.
Designed by architect
Samuel Sloane in 1860,
its construction was
interrupted by the
Civil War; the ornate
mansion/museum was
never completed.*

Plantation House to Marble Palace

More than two centuries separate Charleston's 700-acre Boone Hall Plantation (at left, 1681), framed by its Avenue of Oaks, from financier Henry Flagler's Whitehall (ceiling detail above) in Palm Beach, Florida. The Carolina coast was among the first Southeastern areas to be developed, by wealthy rice planters. Flagler didn't discover potential in the mosquito-plagued Atlantic coast of Florida, which he envisioned as the American Riviera, until 1883. He spent almost $5 million on Whitehall, the centerpiece of opulent Palm Beach. Architects Carrere & Hastings designed the seventy-three-room mansion, which incorporates French Renaissance features like this carved and gilded ceiling. (See also page 134.)

Early Twentieth-Century Revival Styles

Antique porcelain is displayed on the ornate mantel of the French Renaissance-style Pittock Mansion, above, in Portland, Oregon (1909–14). Built by Henry Pittock, the founder of the *Daily Oregonian*, it commands a site a thousand feet above the city and has been restored and furnished in period decor. On the opposite page is the fortresslike Ames estate (1910), built in the popular Tudor Revival style, with terra-cotta pots capping the ivy-covered chimney and a paved forecourt framed by Classical urns. Completely fireproof, the stone mansion stands in Borderland State Park, North Easton, Massachusetts.

Post-Civil War Estates *Overleaf*
The Herndon Home, in Atlanta, Georgia (page 122), combines patterned brickwork and a soaring white portico with an elegant balustrade that extends around the roofline like a crown. Atlanta rose from its ashes to become the South's premier financial and cultural center. On page 123, a tranquil view of the formal gardens at Hildene, in Manchester, Vermont, from the sitting room of this classic Georgian Revival house, built by Robert Todd Lincoln, the eldest son of the nation's best-loved president, in the early 1900s. The twenty-four-room house and grounds in the Battenkill Valley have been restored as a Lincoln family memorial.

Expansive Houses of Brick and Stone

Bellingrath, in Turner, Alabama (above), was designed by architect George B. Rogers for businessman Walter D. Bellingrath during the 1930s, using pre–Civil War bricks, antique wrought ironwork, and art treasures from around the world. A harmonious blend of Colonial, English, and Mediterranean influences, the house has one of the Deep South's most beautiful gardens—sixty acres in almost continuous bloom, modeled on the European formal gardens visited by the Bellingraths in 1927. The English-style manor house on the opposite page, modestly called "Bourn Cottage" by mining tycoon William Bourn Jr., was designed by San Francisco architect Willis Polk in 1897. Native fieldstone, brick, redwood, and cedar were the building materials for this estate house in California's Empire Mine State Historic Park in Nevada County. It bears a resemblance to the famous Red House designed by English architect Philip Webb for William Morris, founder of the Arts and Crafts Movement, in 1859.

Lavish Continental Decor

The richly multitextured and multicolored Music Room above, in Milwaukee's Pabst Mansion (1892), was furnished entirely from a seventeenth-century Bavarian castle by brewer Frederick Pabst. At the Rhine House (opposite), in California's Napa Valley, vintner Frederick Beringer sought to re-create his family home in Mainz, Germany. Stained-glass windows like these set into the double entry door were executed painstakingly in the Belgian Art Nouveau style.

Solitary Splendor *Overleaf*

Maryhill Museum of Art, formerly the Samuel Hill residence, overlooks the parched slopes of the Columbia River Gorge, where Hill hoped to found a colony of fellow Quakers in Goldendale, Washington. This proved impossible, but the wealthy entrepreneur and art collector chose to live here, in a spacious castlelike house designed by architects Hornblower & Marshall in 1914. Poured-concrete construction on a steel I-beam frame make this an unusually modern execution of a period style.

Elegant Townhouses

Above, one of the Classical Charleston, South Carolina, houses on historic East Battery Street shows the combined influences of the post-Revolutionary Adam style and British colonists from the West Indies, who favored broad piazzas at every level for coolness. At left, this Beaux-Arts San Francisco mansion was built by Adolph Spreckels (1857–1924), who made his fortune in the sugar industry. Paired fluted columns flank Palladian windows and upper-level balconies replete with cherubs, swags, and garlands in high relief.

Masonry Palazzos

The eclectic North-Evans Chateau above (1874), in Austin, Texas, combines Romanesque rusticated stonework and deep arches with a flat roof in the Classical style, articulated by a dentiled cornice line. Opposite, Roman villas of the Italian Renaissance era inspired Richard Morris Hunt's 1893 design for The Breakers, Cornelius Vanderbilt II's seventy-room summer cottage in fashionable Newport, Rhode Island. Built at a cost of $7 million, it is the largest house on opulent five-mile Bellevue Avenue—a source of great satisfaction to Vanderbilt, who thereby eclipsed the splendid Chateau-style "house next door" on Ochre Point, which was built by Ogden Goelet.

Showcases for Art Treasures

Whitehall (above), now the Henry Morrison Flagler
Museum (see also page 119), has seventy-three rooms,
including this grand salon in the style of Louis XVI,
with its carved marble fireplace, domed and painted ceiling, and intricate wall panels, reliefs, and moldings. On
the opposite page is a graceful colonnade facing into the
central courtyard at Vizcaya, built on Miami's Biscayne
Bay for James Deering, heir to the International
Harvester fortune, in the 1910s. European art treasures
of nineteen centuries were imported to furnish this nine-
million-dollar estate, designed by architects F. Burrall
Hoffman Jr. and Paul Chalfin in the Venetian-palace
style, with influences from Spain and the French Riviera.
It is now the Dade County Art Museum.

Commanding Prospects

On the opposite page is Biltmore, the Chateauesque-style mansion designed by Richard Morris Hunt for George W. Vanderbilt in 1895. Trained at the Parisian École des Beaux-Arts, Hunt drew upon three centuries of Renaissance design and detailing to create this castle in the Blue Ridge Mountains, near Asheville, North Carolina. Its 250 rooms overlook formal gardens and landscaping by Frederick Law Olmsted, the co-creator, with Calvert Vaux, of New York City's Central Park. The house above is Lyndhurst, at Tarrytown, in New York's lower Hudson Valley. A pre-eminent example of

the Gothic Revival style, it was designed by Alexander Jackson Davis with flush-cut stone walls, romantic towers, medieval-style chimneys, and stone tracery modeled on the ornamentation of European castles and cathedrals.

Overleaf: The rambling *hacienda* of flamboyant "Death Valley Scotty," who rode with Annie Oakley in Buffalo Bill's Wild West Show. A native of Kentucky who struck it rich during the Gold Rush, Walter Perry Scott left a lasting imprint on California's Death Valley with his Mediterranean castle of red-tiled roofs, which combines Moorish, Spanish, Italian, and Mexican motifs.

Medieval Aspirations

The De La Salle Mansion in Newport, Rhode Island (above), has the curvilinear stepped gable, often called the Flemish gable, characteristic of the Low Countries. One of countless historic houses in this port city, which flourished from the early 1600s, it shares the spirit of the Middle Ages with the castle built by Swedish-born Swan J. Turnblad in Minneapolis, Minnesota (1907), as seen by the stained-glass window at right. Imported from Sweden at a cost of $15,000, it depicts the sacking of Gotland's capital, whose conquerer demands tribute of gold, silver, and jewelry.

Palm Beach Personified *Overleaf*
Mar-a-Lago (Sea to Lake), built by Post cereal heiress Marjorie Merriwether Post, is a 118-room pleasure palace in the Hispano-Moorish style, designed in 1923 by Marion Sims Wyeth and Joseph Urban. Its seventy-five-foot tower overlooks a vista extending from the Atlantic to Lake Worth.

Vernacular Styles

Above: A palmetto-frond
shelter indigenous to
the Hawaiian Islands,
created for the Polynesian
Cultural Center at
Laie, Oahu.

Previous pages: The
remnants of Ashcroft,
Colorado, a silver-mining
town constructed, like its
mineshafts, of timber,
during the 1880s. Note
the typically Western
false-front structures
on the right.

By the end of the Civil War in 1865,
a number of regional vernacular
styles were established or evolving
in different parts of North America. Some
had their origins in the colonial styles of
the areas longest settled; others developed
to meet conditions in new areas of population growth, including the Plains, the
Rocky Mountains, the Southwest, and
the West Coast, from southern California
to British Columbia.

Most of these styles were practical,
unpretentious, and relatively easy to build
from available materials. Although many
of them evolved during the Victorian Era
(1830s–early 1900s), they were little
affected by the many fads and fashions
of that period, which are discussed in
detail in the following chapter.

Shacks and shanties of various kinds
provided temporary and low-income
housing from southern Georgia, where
they were built by poor sharecroppers, to
the mining and lumber camps of the
trans-Mississippi West region. A typical
tarpaper shanty consisted of a single room

walled by wide boards and covered by
a wooden roof to which tarpaper was
nailed as weatherproofing. A sheet-metal
stovepipe served as a chimney. Such shelters often incorporated second-hand
materials including doors, boards, and
window frames. Some were transient, others permanent, in which case they might
be enlarged by lean-tos, porches, and
chimneys as a rural family grew larger, if
not richer. Many shanties and cabins were
roofed with galvanized sheet metal from
the mid-nineteenth century onward.

Variations on the English Cottage style
in its simplest form were popularized by
several pattern books, including A.J.
Davis's *Rural Residences* (1837), Gervase
Wheeler's *Rural Homes* (1851), and
Calvert Vaux's *Villas and Cottages* (1857).
Simple, affordable designs, new steam-
powered tools, and the development of
balloon framing with boards cut to standard lengths made these modest homes
available to working- and middle-class
families. Board-and-batten siding and
shingled gabled roofs gave such one- or
two-story houses a rustic look, and
porches became fixtures on Northern
houses, as well as Southern, to increase
outdoor living space during the summer
months and promote the "healthful airs"
that were widely recommended by nineteenth-century authorities.

In mountainous wooded areas, the Swiss
chalet became a popular model for picturesque cottages built of rough-cut lumber, with several balconies and porches
supported by hewn hardwood posts. Wide
eaves and exterior siding cut to resemble
Swiss post-and-beam construction made
an attractive weathertight house in areas
subject to snowfall. Minus the livestock
housed on the ground floor of its Swiss

prototypes, the Chalet style had many admirers, and its influence can still be seen in ski lodges and other winter recreation centers from Vermont to Colorado.

Log cabins and houses were still being built throughout the nineteenth century. Second- and third-generation examples usually had plank floors instead of tamped earth, and larger gaps between the timbers, which were often chinked with cement. Alternatively, the entire log structure might be clad with shingles or with weatherboards. Such houses were commonly seen from the southern Appalachians to Wyoming and Texas, where they still figure in modest ranches and farmsteads; others have been preserved as reminders of local heritage. They have served as models for the prefabricated vacation homes available on today's market, which are constructed much like the Lincoln Log houses that were familiar to generations of children. In the Southwest, the Navajo still construct their traditional octagonal *hogans* of logs, sometimes banked into a hillside.

Another informal style that became popular after the California Gold Rush of 1849 was the false-front structure. The Main Streets of many new towns unified their simple gable- and shed-roofed buildings by adding a rectangular wooden façade that rose above the gable to create the flat-roofed look of the Italianate style in older towns and cities. Essentially, the false front, as is seen in so many Western movies, unified the disparate shapes of commercial and residential buildings and made them appear larger and more significant. These façades were especially popular in the farming and mining communities that began to spring up in Nevada, Colorado, Montana, and other Mountain states.

In the Midwest, a distinct vernacular style had emerged by the end of the nineteenth century. It is exemplified in the two-story rectangular brick house with an off-center entrance, front-facing gable, sash widows with segmental (slightly arched) heads, and, in many cases, an L-shaped extension with its own gable. This basic plan was ornamented in various styles over time, from modest Greek Revival pediments and friezes to Gothic arches, Italianate brackets, cupolas, "gingerbread" trim, and other fashionable modes, but the plan remained the same and is still characteristic of the region.

Below: Chili peppers hung to dry brighten the courtyard of the timber-framed Martinez Adobe in Taos, New Mexico, site of the nation's oldest continuously inhabited town, Taos Pueblo.

Above: A gable-roofed farmstead overlooks the rich, furrowed land of Argyle Shores, Prince Edward Island, where many industrious Scots settled.

Florida was one of the last states to be settled widely, and its distinctive architecture draws upon Spanish Colonial, Mediterranean, and Caribbean styles, including the picturesque houses of Key West, which were modeled upon those of the Bahamas. They were designed to withstand high winds in seasonal hurricanes, and have wide porches supported by slender columns for maximum ventilation (Key West is the southernmost point of the United States). The island's high-pitched roofs took this form to funnel much-needed rainwater into cisterns. John James Audubon lived here in 1832, while painting *The Birds of the Keys*, and writer Ernest Hemingway and his wife occupied the former Asa Tift house—Spanish style with French decorative ele-

ments—in 1931–40. It is now a museum and a National Historic Landmark.

Spanish St. Augustine, after it was burned by the British in the early eighteenth century, replaced its original palm-thatched shelters with masonry buildings of coquina, the native shell-rock, which was plastered over to repel dampness. In Pensacola, also founded by the Spanish, the Gulf Coast and French West Indian styles are prominent, with many houses built of brick with oyster-shell mortar. Tampa, too, bears the imprint of Spain, combined with that of Cuban and Italian immigrants who came here from 1886 to work in the local cigar industry. The backwoods of northern Florida and the Panhandle are still dotted with moss-draped cabins and shanties built by settlers of the Territory before it became a state. Future president Andrew Jackson served as the first territorial governor in this sparsely populated region, where the sultry climate and limited building materials resulted in vernacular architecture typical of the Deep South.

The southern Louisiana bayou country retains its Cajun and Creole heritage in the one- and two-story raised cottages, usually two rooms deep, with an integral porch under a steep roofline, either straight or flared. The prevalence of flooding in this low-lying area of the Mississippi Delta also made houseboats a popular—as well as mobile—form of dwelling. The French Colonial urban cottages of New Orleans were still being constructed long after the Louisiana Purchase of 1803, and modified versions, with lacy wrought-iron balconies and cobblestoned inner courtyards, are still seen in the city's *Vieux Carré*. The state capital, upriver at Baton Rouge (or Red Stick), shows Spanish as well as French influences, including the Pino-Charlet House (1821) and the Stewart-Dougherty House (1848), which are both located in what is called Spanish Town.

As mentioned earlier, Southwestern architecture is still readily recognizable as an amalgam of Spanish Colonial, Mexican, Native American, and Anglo forms adapted to the region's arid climate and varied topography. The Territorial style in New Mexico, west Texas, and Arizona is seen in flat-roofed, single-story houses with a crown of brick, rather than adobe, along the parapet, and a front porch, rather than the back porch of earlier times. Wooden detailing in various nineteenth-century styles was also added by Anglo settlers in this region. In southern California, the first American settlers built shedlike frame houses with overhanging eaves and roofs covered with tar (later, shingles or sheet metal). Few of these dwellings have survived the twentieth-century population explosion in the Los Angeles metropolitan area, which is now an eclectic blend of Spanish Colonial, Bungalow, Mediterranean, Art Deco, Beach House, and assorted other period and Modern styles.

From the 1830s, northern California's Monterey style evolved under the auspices of New Englander Thomas O. Larkin, who had a major impact on the city's development into a "Yankee" port reached by sailing around the Horn of South America. A regional variant on the two-story New England Colonial-style house, Larkin's residence was a two-story adobe with a hipped roof and balconies along both levels of the front and sides. Other immigrants emulated this style in various ways. Some built a cantilevered second-floor porch that served to shade the ground floor, and reverted to the familiar long gable roof, covered by red tile attached to wooden rafters. Others added shutters for more shade and covered the roof with hand-split shingles in New England fashion. Interior staircases replaced the indigenous exterior stairs to balconies, a feature of both French and Spanish styles. Single-story Monterey houses retained the full-length porch along the façade. The style became popular statewide, and it would serve as a prototype for Modern architecture in California a century later.

Below: The Laramore-Lyman House (1870), with its neat white trim and metal roof, is part of California's Fresno Flats State Historic Park, in Oakhurst.

Above: A tranquil house-boat community on the east side of Lake Union, in Seattle, Washington. The innumerable waterways of the Puget Sound area make boating a way of life here.

In Canada, first France, then England made profound impressions on the built landscape. In Quebec City, the cradle of French civilization in the Americas, extensive restoration has been done to the seventeenth- and eighteenth-century masonry buildings of the Place Royale, along the St. Lawrence Riverfront. Samuel de Champlain built his fortified "Habitation" here in 1608—the oldest French building on its original site in North America. From this nucleus, French settlers, called *habitants*, built wooden farmsteads modeled on those of the homeland, often forming a U-shaped enclosure, or a wholly enclosed court-

yard, in the styles of Normandy and Brittany for protection against the weather. Townhouses like those seen in Trois-Rivières, founded in 1634 some seventy-five miles from Quebec City, have steeply pitched gabled roofs, short pentroofs above the ground-floor façade, and multiple dormer windows at the second-story level. Few of the original frame buildings have survived, but fieldstone walls plastered over with whitewash or stucco to protect the joints proved an enduring feature of Eastern Canadian architecture. Similar houses may be seen in Old Montreal, contrasting with the Neoclassical, French Second Empire, and other residential styles of a later date in this beautiful and historic port.

Acadia was the name France gave to what we now call Atlantic Canada, and some of the Acadians expelled from this area by the British in 1755 eventually returned and took up their simple way of life, which has been reconstructed in New Brunswick's Acadian Village. Fishing and farming were the principal occupations here, where the oldest house dates back to 1797; other dwellings have been moved from Fredericton, Edmundston, and other parts of New Brunswick. Nova Scotia was settled largely, as its name suggests, by Scots, who built sturdy frame houses with multiple gables, or masonry cottages in the compact Celtic style, usually whitewashed inside and out.

Many of the original French residents of Fortress Louisbourg, on Cape Breton Island, were highly skilled masons, metalworkers, and carpenters—a legacy that has been restored to life at the Fortress of Louisbourg National Historic Park, where much of the town founded in 1720 has been reconstructed. The original complex was so expensive that King Louis XV—a prodigal spender by any standard—complained that he expected to see the fort's ten-foot-thick walls looming over the French horizon.

English settlers of Newfoundland and Prince Edward Island built rectangular, steep-roofed gabled houses and seaside cottages, often covered with weatherboard or shingles. Vernacular styles here have much in common with New England, as seen in the many saltbox-style houses and barns—often painted white, with red trimwork—on Prince Edward Island, where the fertility of the soil and the beauty of the gently rolling landscape exert a compelling attraction on residents and visitors alike.

In Ontario, brick clay was readily available and commonly utilized, along with native wood and stone. This province—Canada's second largest—became a rich source of grain and other agricultural products for the nation and, later, its principal manufacturing area. Major settlement occurred after the Revolutionary War, when colonists loyal to England immigrated by the thousands, bringing their own vernacular building styles into the area. In many cases, whole communities relocated, including Pennsylvania Dutch and Mennonite pacifists. Most other nineteenth-century arrivals were Scottish or English, and ties with the United States were strengthened in 1829, when the Welland Canal opened to link the Great Lakes shipping channels with the St. Lawrence River. After World War I, an influx of immigrants from Finland and Scandinavia contributed new ethnic styles to the still-growing province, which experienced major immigration from Europe after World War II.

Both Manitoba and Alberta were still sparsely settled frontier areas in the late nineteenth century, dotted with ranches and farms like those of the American West. The province of Manitoba was not created until 1870, when the newly formed Dominion of Canada (1867) reached an agreement with the British government and the Hudson's Bay Company, which had domain over all the northern territory (known as Rupert's Land) draining into Hudson Bay. The Pacific Coast colony of British Columbia, which included Vancouver Island after 1866, became the sixth province of the Dominion in 1871, when the government agreed to link the region to the East Coast by rail. The architectural influence of Victorian England is most apparent in British Columbia, where the cities of Vancouver and Victoria soon emerged as major Pacific ports. Its milder climate and cultural ties to the North American West Coast contributed to the region's distinctive—sometimes flamboyant—architecture, as seen in the following chapter.

Below: Tropical plants and a gravel-edged brick path frame Simonton Court, a Bahamas-style enclave in Key West, Florida, with gabled board-and-batten cottages.

Guardians of the Land

On the previous pages, a colorful hip-roofed farmhouse
and a spacious Pennsylvania-style barn stand between
field and sea in the town of Souris, Prince Edward
Island. The multigabled house above, flanked by shed-
roofed porches, has a hilltop view of surrounding vineyards near Santa Rosa, California. On the opposite page,
burgeoning crops are a welcome sight from this whitewashed Gothic-style cottage, with modest Victorian
gablework, in North Wiltshire, Prince Edward Island.

Picturesque and Unpretentious

Timber construction takes very different forms in these contrasting structures. The attractive two-story house above, in a modified Chalet style, overlooks the rolling countryside north of San Francisco. On the opposite page, a rough-hewn log cabin in Old Baylor Park, Independence, Texas, speaks only to shelter, with a humble beauty of its own.

Second-generation Western Homes

The historic Oneto House, at left, in Amador County, California, has narrow galleries with timber supports and a detached brick kitchen (more often seen in the South). Above is a substantial fenced log house with twin chimneys and a single dormer, built by Joseph Bird in Round Mountain, Texas, in 1858.

Harmonious Notes in the Landscape

The Creole-style Laura Plantation House above, in Vacherie, Louisiana (1805), is typical of the dwellings built by French planters along the Mississippi. Open to the air on all sides, the house seems to merge with its tree-shaded grounds. On the opposite page is the Sanders Home in Volcano, California, a two-story house combining Bungalow and Monterey-style features. The sizable addition on the right conforms to the scenic hillside setting, with its bright cascade of California poppies.

Handsome Piazzas, Town and Country

Above, a white-faced Hereford and a patch of blue-bonnets are clues to the location of the Brandenburg Ranch House in Hilda, Texas, built of multicolored native stone. Slender columns and a second-story balustrade extend the full width of the façade. On the opposite page, a gracious Savannah, Georgia, town-house (1881), raised on brick piers, takes advantage of every cooling breeze with its intricately detailed Victorian-style galleries inspired by Classical forms.

Gold-Rush False-fronts Surrender to Time

Permafrost activity has undermined these buildings in Dawson City, Yukon Territory, dating from the Klondike Gold Rush. Now leaning at drunken angles, they are remnants of the "City of Gold" that sprang up here a hundred years ago. Most of the riotous old mining town has been restored, including the flamboyant Palace Grand Theatre and Diamond Tooth Gertie's Gambling Hall.

Living History, Midwest *Overleaf*
On page 166, a nineteenth-century farmhouse pantry, faithfully replicated in Urbandale, Iowa. On page 167, a modest clapboard house in Greenfield Village, near Dearborn, Michigan, where automobile manufacturer Henry Ford established the nation's largest indoor-outdoor museum complex to "reproduce American life as lived."

Winds of Change

Above, a solitary log wall with diagonal bracing looks out on the shadowed San Miguel Mountains in the Colorado ghost town of Alta Mines. At left, an abandoned farmhouse in Blomidon, Nova Scotia, harbors only its memories. On the following pages, lonely houses typical of those built by miners in Telluride, Colorado.

Mountainous Footholds *Previous pages*

On page 172, a tiny white bungalow appears as a dot on the steeply descending landscape of the Trinity Alps, in California's Trinity National Forest. On page 173, the Enchanted Valley Chalet, in Olympic National Park, Washington, built by the U.S. Forest Service in 1931 to house hikers and riders in the Olympic Mountains. Now owned by the National Park Service, it stands in a meadow backed by a precipitous rock wall some 2,000 feet high.

North to Alaska

The countless tidal inlets and swift-running streams of the forty-ninth state dictate houses raised on stilts, or piers, as seen above, and opposite, in Ketchikan. The scarcity of roads in this vast area—one of whose glaciers is larger than Switzerland—means that most settlements are close to the coastline and nonlocal building materials are delivered by ferry. Thus many vernacular structures have a rough-and-ready improvised quality.

Unmistakably New Orleans

The pastel-painted brick townhouse above, with lou-
vered doors and wrought-iron balcony, embodies the
spirit of the old French Quarter. At right is the famous
cast-iron morning glory and cornstalk fence designed
for Colonel Robert H. Short's ninteenth-century villa
in the city's historic Garden District.

Foursquare Shelter *Overleaf*
A weathered frame structure holds its own under a lowering sky streaked with birds in California's Fall River Valley farmland.

The Victorian Era

Above: A wide verandah framed by graceful latticework encircles this clapboard Victorian, with its patriotic roof ornament, in Sutter Creek, California, where the Gold Rush began.

Previous pages: Beautifully restored Queen Anne Revival-style townhouses on San Francisco's historic Alamo Square.

Throughout the nineteenth century, in both Europe and North America, what has been called "the Battle of the Styles"—Classical and Gothic—was fully joined, with the balance shifting first toward one, then to the other. As the British authors of *The History of Architecture* (1950) point out, "Miscellaneous minor revivals allied themselves with each [side]. The revival of Classic architecture, whether Greek, Graeco-Roman, or Renaissance, was by no means exhausted by mid-century, but it is a reasonable generalisation to say that it then lost place for a while to the mediaeval as the dominant practice. After 1880, Classicism returned again to the higher favour in most kinds of building except the ecclesiastic."

In the United States, this process is illustrated by the career of architect Benjamin H. Latrobe, who designed the nation's first Greek Revival building—Philadelphia's Bank of Pennsylvania—in 1801. However, Latrobe was also instrumental in introducing the Gothic Revival style, in 1818, when he submitted alternate Classical and Gothic designs for Baltimore's Cathedral of the Assumption. His Classical plan was preferred, but many architects were inspired by his Gothic Revival work, which became the dominant form in ecclesiastical architecture by mid-century. Thus the two major influences that we associate with the Victorian house were, in fact, established here several decades before the young British queen began her reign in 1837 and persisted for years after her death in 1901. In addition, many styles that have been loosely described as "Victorian" because of their chronology, including the mid-century French Empire style, were quite independent of Victorian England in origin and inspiration.

Although the period was markedly eclectic, especially after the American Civil War, there are commonalities of both style and spirit underlying the apparent diversity of the age. The Industrial Revolution, improvements in both transportation and communication, growing prosperity among the middle class, and an emphasis on personal expression through residential architecture all played a part. So did Victorian notions of good order, healthful location, the importance of family life, and more flexible living spaces. Comfort was valued highly, along with privacy and the pursuit of a multitude of new interests, from cultivating newly discovered plants to collecting souvenirs of one's travels and displaying them prominently. More leisure time, for many people, meant wider reading, new ideas, a greater willingness to experiment, and a deeper awareness of the larger world. These qualities were fostered by the first great "world's fairs," including London's Crystal Palace Exhibition of 1851, the Philadelphia Centennial of 1876, and the Neoclassical "White City" built for Chicago's World's Columbian Exposition in 1893.

In domestic architecture, the Early Gothic Revival was imported from England during the 1830s. Its British champions included the influential architect Augustus W.N. Pugin, who made the case for medieval over Classical architecture in his book *Contrasts*, published in 1836. The idea that a man's home (however modest) was his castle gained impetus with Pugin's ideas on asymmetrical houses whose designs conformed to the contours of the site and the owner's personal needs and plans, rather than conforming the residents to a rigid, unyielding plan dictated by Classical modes. In fact, this was an early version of Frank Lloyd Wright's vow to "break out of the box" with designs in which form and function were one. However, Pugin's views harked back to medieval antecedents, as would John Ruskin's. The latter's major works, including *The Stones of Venice* and *The Seven Lamps of Architecture*, which looked to Italian rather than English Gothic models, had a major impact not only upon the late-century High Victorian Gothic style, but on British and American proponents of the Arts and Crafts Movement, as discussed more fully in the following chapter. Another influential British architect and writer was Robert Kerr, the author of *The Gentleman's House; or How to Plan English Residences from the Parsonage to the Palace* (1864). Both in America and Canada, architects studied these works

Below: A spacious cubic Italianate with a rooftop balustrade, the Lake House, in Reno, Nevada, recalls the state's glory days as a fast-growing mining frontier.

avidly, and the houses they designed for wealthy clients found their less expensive counterparts through plans and pattern books like those of Alexander Jackson Davis and his colleague Andrew Jackson Downing. The latter's *Cottage Residences* (1842) reached a vast audience among those newly awakened to the delights of the "picturesque" in buildings and landscaping. Davis strove for the ideal house by combining steeply sloped roofs, balconies, gables, porches, and old-style casement windows in rambling plans on attractive sites; they could be added to and altered as a family increased, or found the need for new kinds of living space.

Below: The French Second Empire Gallagher House (1882), with lacelike ornamentation — a landmark in the historic resort of Cape May, New Jersey, which has some six hundred notable Victorians.

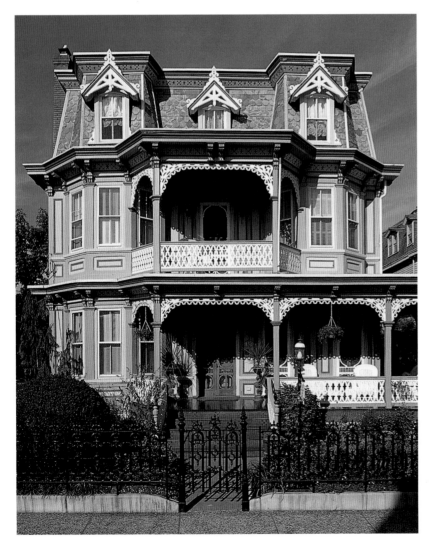

Another distinctive and extremely popular style of the day was the Italianate, inspired by Renaissance models. Queen Victoria herself was captivated by it, as seen in the Italian villa-style Osborne House (1845), a country house on the Isle of Wight codesigned by her husband, Prince Albert of Saxe-Coburg, and the London architect Thomas Cubitt. It featured asymmetrically placed towers in the square, bracketed Tuscan mode and stucco facing, with a floor plan that included public and private wings. On a smaller scale, the style found favor for country and suburban houses across North America, while its "city cousin," the cubic Italianate townhouse, or brownstone, lined the streets of New York, Boston, Philadelphia, and San Francisco. A mid-century view of New York City south of 36th Street shows entire blocks of three- and four-story examples — usually attached, rather than freestanding, and ornamented with detailing inspired by the Italian Renaissance. These themes would be reprised later in the century by the first generation of American architects to study at the classically oriented École des Beaux-Arts.

Some of our best-loved Victorians breathe the spirit of the Tuscan villa, which combined square massing with a horizontal emphasis, campaniles and cupolas, arched windows, and large brackets, often paired, below the cornice line. Such a house was designed by the New Haven architect Henry Austin for hotel proprietor Ruggles S. Morse in Portland, Maine (1858). Purchased by entrepreneur Joseph R. Libby in 1893, the Morse-Libby House is widely considered the finest in the Italian-villa style still standing in the United States. Like the urban brownstones, it was constructed of brick faced with sandstone, and its richly appointed interiors are attributed to designer Gustave Herter. Countless other examples have been preserved by local historical societies and landmark preservation groups, and some have been maintained by their original owners as private dwellings; resort homes, as seen in Cape May, New Jersey, a National Historic Landmark City; and bed-and-breakfast inns of informal charm for escapees from the pace of urban life today.

Another popular period style, as mentioned above, was the French Second Empire, which was readily combined with the Italianate. Its hallmark is the mansard roofline—a two-sloped hipped roof with dormer windows on the lower slope, often framed by ornate surrounds. The slopes may be concave, convex, straight, or a combination thereof. This was a contemporary style in the 1850s, inspired by the designs of Emperor Napoleon III and Baron Hausmann, who replaced many medieval Paris streets with wide, tree-lined boulevards and imposing national monuments during the emperor's reign (1851–70). Here, too, international exhibitions held in the newly resplendent Paris (1855 and 1867) inspired North American visitors, and the "French roof" became such a popular feature that it was used to crown vernacular houses in a variety of other styles. In its most authentic form, the Second Empire-style house also boasted ornate door and window surrounds, iron cresting along the eaves and/or roofline, and porches and balconies with handsome balustrades. Some examples also sprouted cupolas or towers along Italianate lines. The style was embraced enthusiastically

in Canada, especially in Quebec, including Montreal, with its long French heritage. In the United States, it became so popular after the Civil War that it was often called the General Grant style, for the presidency of the military hero who came to the White House in 1869.

The indigenous Stick style featured elements adapted from medieval English building traditions and translated into the American vernacular. As named and described by architectural historian Vincent Scully, it featured a style of patterning on wood-frame houses inspired by picturesque English prototypes, whereby the wooden armature of the house was brought to the surface and articulated by embellishments including

Above: A side-facing stickwork gable and a corner tower crowned by a "witch's cap" roof with finial are typical Queen Anne Revival features, seen here in Hoquiam, Washington.

Above: The Tudor Revival style became immensely popular during the late nineteenth century, when oriel windows, medieval chimneys, and "half-timbered" gables sprang up across the nation. This handsome example is in Pittsburgh, Pennsylvania.

diagonal braces, rippling effects, and rhythmic vertical and horizontal moldings. As Mr. Scully observes in his introduction to *The Architecture of the American Summer* (Rizzoli, 1989): "Andrew Jackson Downing and a horde of builders of single-family houses from Maine to California could even achieve the new effects…with vertical planks and battens alone." Transitional between the Gothic Revival and the Queen Anne styles, this would figure largely in the latter, with

ornamental stickwork used to pleasing effect on many of the late-century "Painted Ladies" that have been so carefully restored in San Francisco and a host of other communities.

Contemporaneous with the Stick style was the Shingle style, a domestic adaptation of the later work of Richard Norman Shaw and other English architects who sought to unify eclectic buildings with new types of cladding and ornamentation. The major American pioneer of this style was Henry Hobson Richardson, whose work incorporated Romanesque elements that would feature largely in his unique Richardsonian Romanesque style of the late 1800s. The Shingle style originated on the East Coast and became very popular for informal, rambling seaside and resort houses that incorporated short, square towers, pronounced arches, hipped roofs, and deep porches. In some cases, unpainted siding alternated with machine-made shingles that were rough-cut to resemble their earlier handmade prototypes. Rusticated masonry foundations and porch supports were a common feature, and in many instances, the whole structure was shingle-clad. The style also gained adherents in the Midwest, including the young Frank Lloyd Wright, who worked on a Shingle-style church during his early days as a draftsman and incorporated many features of the style in his first home/studio, in Oak Park, Illinois. Rare examples may also be found on the West Coast; more often, Shingle-style elements were incorporated into the triumphant late-century Queen Anne Revival style.

The High Victorian, or Ruskinian Gothic, style drew upon the principles enunciated by John Ruskin, especially the use of contrasting surface materials, called polychrome, that made color and pattern an intrinsic part of the building. In its pure form, this style was used mainly for churches, public buildings, and expensive masonry estate houses like those illustrated in chapter 4. However, wooden counterparts in residential architecture adopted the multitextured and multicolored features of this English vernacular style for the Queen Anne Revival house that is often considered the quintessential Victorian in the United States and Canada. Americans were introduced to this style of architecture at Philadelphia's Centennial Exposition of 1876, and it soon spread nationwide.

Imaginative, fanciful, and highly individual, this culmination of the Victorian styles incorporated a bewildering variety of plans and detailing, but underlying themes included spacious floor plans, large porches to serve as outdoor sitting rooms, and carefully tended landscapes inspired by Britain's Garden Suburb aesthetic. Eaves, porches, and cornice lines were ornamented with spindle- and spoolwork, scroll-sawn gingerbread trim, pendants and finials, elaborate bargeboards, and stickwork. Conical turrets, wide eaves, carved brackets, and multiple gables added visual interest, with disparate elements united into a pleasing whole by intricate paintwork involving four to six harmonious colors alternating with ornamental shingle and appliqué work, from carved reliefs and friezes to terra-cotta panels featuring naturalistic motifs. Combining both picturesque and Classical features, including pediments, pilasters, and columns, the exuberant Queen Anne Revival house represented, to its many admirers, a resolution to the century-long "Battle of the Styles."

***Below:** A rambling Shingle-style resort house, with shed dormers, multi-level porches, and a view of the sea from Rhode Island's Watch Hill.*

Summer Places

Decorative scrollwork converges on a pendant over a gabled balcony (above) at the Oak Bluffs Camp Ground in Martha's Vineyard, Massachusetts, a picturesque enclave of the Carpenter Gothic style. On the opposite page is an airy spindle- and spoolwork porch on Mackinac Island, Michigan, which became a popular watering place during the late 1800s. Long before that, statesman William Cullen Bryant had praised its "delightful climate during the summer months" and the "grateful coolness" of its southwest winds.

Vintage Dream Houses

The gracious Queen Anne above, built in Westport, Connecticut, in 1899, has all the amenities prized by Victorian-era families: well-kept lawns, wraparound verandahs, surprising nooks and crannies, and room to grow. Opposite, Cape May's venerable Joseph Hall House (1868), an exemplar of the Carpenter Gothic style, with its finely detailed bargeboards, dormers, brackets, and scrollwork.

Rhythmic Motifs

Repeating patterns unify the elements of the colorful Savannah, Georgia, rowhouses above and the façades of Victorian Ferndale, California (at right), fronted by wrought-iron hitching posts.

Masonry Treatments *Overleaf*

A curving gated stairway opens to a view of the stately Harris-Cameron House (page 194), in Harrisburg, Pennsylvania, a symmetrical Georgian-style residence to which the arched porch was added at a later date — typical of the period. On page 195, also in Harrisburg, is the J. Donald Cameron House, an eclectic blend of Gothic, Italianate, and Second Empire elements in which the round-headed windows and bracketed eaves strike a harmonious chord.

Townhouses in the Grand Manner

Savannah's Mercer House (above), built in the mid-1800s, combines Italianate elements like the bracketed cornice line with an unusually ornate pediment over the French doors onto the balcony. It is solidly constructed of the warmly colored local brick. At right is New York City's Gramercy Park West, part of a handsome complex of Italianate brownstones surrounding a private park to which the residents hold the keys—the last such enclave in Manhattan today.

Freely Combined Styles

The mid-century "French" or mansard roof was often added to an earlier house like the one at left, built by a steamboat captain in Boonville, Missouri, in 1800. Patterned slate was the preferred material. The Romanesque Revival house above, called Open Gates, was built in Galveston, Texas, before the great hurricane and flood of 1900. It has an unusual steeply pitched hipped roof of French Renaissance inspiration.

Local Color

Above, a fanciful Newport, Rhode Island, summer house complete with mansard roofline, gingerbread trim, and wooden corner quoins painted to simulate cut stone. At right, Glen Auburn, built by Natchez, Mississippi, merchant Simon Moses during the late nineteenth century—a handsome counterpoint to the city's many prebellum plantation houses.

Second Empire Angles *Overleaf*

Masonry townhouses (page 202) crowned by Second Empire rooflines in Montreal, Canada, a bastion of French culture in the New World since the early 1600s. On page 203, the asymmetrical villa-style roofline of Glenview House, a landmark of the lower Hudson Valley, now serving as the Hudson River Museum of Westchester County.

Fresh Inspirations *Pages 204–205*

The Petaluma Riverfront in Sonoma County, California, and a delightful, ornate Rocky Mountain cottage in Georgetown, Colorado, illustrate the diversity of Victorian detailing.

House Proud *Previous pages*

Starrett House (1889, page 206), in Port Townsend, Washington's, Historic District, is a classic Carpenter Gothic built by a local sawmill operator. It was called the "House of Four Seasons" because of the frescoes decorating the domed ceiling of the entrance hall. Now an inn, it retains an indoor widow's walk in the tower and a free-hung spiral staircase with carved banisters and balusters incorporating five different woods. On page 207, roofline details of The Abbey, one of Cape May's best-loved Victorians, which has also found new life as an inn for today's travelers.

Lacy Ornamentation

Above, an impeccable "Painted Lady" in Ferndale, California, the well-named Gingerbread Mansion is graced with every feature of the Queen Anne style, from picturesque corner tower to multitextured cladding, intricate spoolwork, "Eastlake-style" gable ornamentation, wrought-iron cresting, bay windows, and double entry door—all painted in the festive colors of a wedding cake. On the opposite page is Cape May's Stockton Cottage, with the second-floor sleeping porch typical of the nineteenth-century seaside resort. The gable is crowned by an intricate acroterion.

Summer's End, Mackinac Island *Previous pages*

The busy waterfront at this scenic Great Lakes crossroads slows its pace as ferryboats and pleasure craft filled with summer visitors leave the island to its permanent residents, who keep to their nineteenth-century ways by forbidding automobiles here. The island's Victorian treasures include the five-story Grand Hotel (1887), the Geary House (1844), and the Mission House and Church on Huron Street, former headquarters of the American Board of Commissioners for Foreign Missions.

California Vineyards

The elegant Queen Anne above is a fitting centerpiece for the Sutter Home Winery at St. Helena, in the Napa Valley. Both European-born and American vintners were drawn to the region's prime grape-growing land during the late nineteenth century, finding the soil types and climate that make the Golden State one of the nation's two great winemaking centers. On the opposite page, a modest villa presides over the luxuriant vines of the Seghesio Winery in Sonoma County's Alexander Valley.

Reaching for the Skies

On the opposite page, a slant-sided bay window with sunburst appliqués, bracketwork, and an exotic pinnacled roof adjoins a basket-arched balcony in Green Bay, Wisconsin. Below, a mansard-crowned dowager with projecting front bay, elaborate hood molds, and a balustraded entry porch in Rockport, Maine.

Eureka!

California's state motto, inspired by the Gold Rush, gave its name to the town of Eureka ("I have found it!"), where lumber magnate William M. Carson built the flamboyant mansion (opposite and above) that became one of the nation's best-known Victorians (1885). Every kind of wood on the world market was used to create the incredibly detailed ornamentation seen here, including appliqué work, finials, bargeboards, balustrades, stick-work, and moldings. The eighteen-room house, crafted by more than a hundred carpenters, is now a private club.

The City Beautiful *Overleaf*

San Francisco has led the nation in preserving the beauty of its Victorian heritage, as seen in the richly ornamented balcony of the landmark house on page 218 and the colorful townhouses on page 219. Built mainly of native redwood, San Francisco's famously attractive townhouses were painted and styled in highly individual ways, with more elaborate ornamentation and paintwork than most of their East Coast counterparts. The city's steep topography adds visual interest, as the houses rise in tiers along the narrow streets.

Early Modernism

Right: Exquisite relief ornamentation on Louis Sullivan's Charnley House (Chicago, 1891), one of the master architect's few residential designs, on which Wright, then an apprentice, collaborated.

Previous pages: Frank Lloyd Wright's Melvyn Maxwell Smith House (1946), in Bloomfield Hills, Michigan, a harmonious series of low geometric planes in the tawny colors of brick and cypress.

Decisive strides into Modern architecture were taken after the great Chicago Fire of 1871, which leveled much of the city. Its role as the new economic center for the Midwest and West made rapid rebuilding imperative, and escalating land values dictated that growth should be upward. The result was the skyscraper, facilitated by the invention of the first safe passenger elevator by Elisha Graves Otis in 1857 and by new techniques for manufacturing rolled steel for framing high-rise buildings.

Architects of the Chicago School, including Louis Sullivan, Daniel H. Burnham, John W. Root, and William Le Baron Jenney, pioneered the construction of tall buildings free of the limitations of masonry and lighted by expanses of glass between steel structural members. Sullivan's mastery of rich, organically inspired ornament, including decorative friezes, is apparent at the façade openings and cornice lines of his commercial buildings, where they created

a sense of continuity. During his partnership with Dankmar Adler, he designed the Charnley House in Chicago, incorporating distinctive woodwork and the use of patterned art glass to create a rhythmic, open interior that combined hand craftsmanship with high-quality machine-made components (1891).

Four years earlier, the young Frank Lloyd Wright had joined the firm and soon became chief draftsman and residential designer. He adopted his mentor's organic style of ornament for the many houses he designed for Chicago businessmen and professionals. However, when he established his own practice, Wright's architecture moved away from restrained urban classicism to multiplaned, horizontal plans in which living spaces interpenetrated one another and were visually anchored to their sites. In his first home/studio at Oak Park, Illinois, he experimented with the looser open forms that resulted in the harmonious, low-level Prairie Houses that won international attention at the turn of the twentieth century. His various plans emanated from a central fireplace core that unified the flexible, family-oriented living areas and related them to the outdoors through balconies set at various levels, bands of casement windows, and wide, overhanging eaves that provided a sense of shelter. Bedrooms and other private spaces were arranged in a series of "zones" that provided for solitude, quiet study, and a sense of repose. Major works of his early period include the Ward W. Willits House (1902), in Highland Park, Illinois; the Darwin Martin House (1904), in Buffalo, New York; and the Avery Coonley House (1909), in River Forest, Illinois. The best-known work of this period is Chicago's

Robie House (1909), which is generally considered the culmination of this style, which Wright described as "organic architecture." Throughout his seventy-year career, in experiments with materials from brick and poured concrete to steel and glass, he sought to create buildings that grew like living organisms in their adaptation to various environments, sites, materials, and uses. Fallingwater, at Bear Run, Pennsylvania (1935), is his residential masterwork.

A romantic and an artist at heart, Wright was among the first Americans to see the possibilities inherent in the British Arts and Craft Movement, which was popularized here, in part, by the English designer C.F.A. Voysey, with whom Wright became friendly. However, he combined the Arts and Crafts ethos with an appreciation for the potential applications of well-made machined articles and experimented tirelessly with new construction techniques and materials. His concerns were wide-ranging and included affordable designs for working-class housing. As early as 1895, he designed Chicago's Francisco Terrace Apartments as an alternative to the dreary rowhouses that he considered unworthy of a democratic society. Francisco Terrace turned its back on the city and overlooked an inner courtyard entered by an impressive arch. The corners of the building housed towers containing both stairways and utilities, with the upper-level apartments accessed by balconies. Such plans would become common during the twentieth century, but they were a distinct innovation at the time.

Several Utopian-style Arts and Crafts communities along British lines were established in the United States, including Roycroft, in East Aurora, New York, and Rose Valley, New York. Set up upon models established in England by C.R. Ashbee and others in the mid-1800s, craftsmen lived and worked in a communal setting, earning modest wages for their goods, including hand-bound books, furniture, and metalwork. Rose Valley architect William Price designed a house for Edward Bok, the editor of the popular *Ladies' Home Journal*, who first gave Frank Lloyd Wright's work national exposure. Bok was a tireless supporter of the Arts and Crafts aesthetic, which gained additional ground when several entrepreneurial designers and architects took a hand.

One moving force was Gustav Stickley, who had trained as an architect before founding his Craftsman furniture workshop in Syracuse, New York, in 1898. Like Wright, Stickley had been impressed by C.R. Ashbee and other founders of the movement, some of whom he met in Europe, but he brought less idealism and more business acumen to his endeavors. Stickley's design magazine *The Craftsman*

Below: Frank Lloyd Wright's first home/studio, in Oak Park, Illinois (1889–1909), which began as a simple Shingle-style house and became an organic work in progress for twenty years.

Above: The Romanesque influence of Henry Hobson Richardson is apparent in Wright's dramatic arched entryway to the Arthur Heurtley House (1902), executed in narrow Roman brick. This early Prairie House was one of the architect's favorites.

reached a wide audience, with mail-order plans for low-cost Bungalow-style houses (called "Craftsman Homes") and advertisements for his plain Mission-style furniture, made of solid oak finished and stained by hand. In the Craftsman house, details were carefully considered, leading to warm, coherent interiors created by the use of built-in furniture; natural materials including redwood, tile, and stone, with earth colors contributing to the overall effect; and unusual stairway treatments.

The affordable Bungalow style, influenced by many factors, including the Japanese teahouse and the Swiss chalet, was the first in the United States to be built in quantity by contractor-builders for speculative sale. From 1905 onward, it spread rapidly throughout the nation, usually in the form of a single-story house with simple lines, projecting eaves, and a large front verandah, often accessed by a stoop. The porch posts were tapered, and some examples had a partial second floor. Various regions adapted the bungalow to seacoast, suburban, or mountain-resort use, and the most elegant houses in this style were built

by California architects Charles and Henry Greene, brothers who established a successful practice in Pasadena. Their low-pitched, multilevel rooflines crowned wooden buildings based entirely on craftsmanship principles, built with the help of Japanese carpenters—mainly of redwood—and featuring exposed roof rafters that were rounded and polished, and open plans extended by balconies and terraces. The Greenes' best-known works include Pasadena's Gamble House (1908) and the Charles M. Pratt House in Nordhoff, California (1909). The latter was built on a fieldstone foundation and had shingle siding stained in earth tones, with gently pitched gable roofs overhanging bands of casement windows. The U-shaped plan followed the contours of the site, with a sleeping porch and two bedrooms on the ground floor, a large living room and dining room open to adjacent terraces, and kitchen and service quarters with a separate entrance. The Greenes oversaw every aspect of construction, fabricating most of their own hardware, decorative tiles, art-glass windows, and furniture, both built-in and movable. Their rich interiors glowed with the luster of teak and mahogany paneling.

Long established as Gothic Revival architects, partners Ralph Adams Cram and Bertram Grosvenor Goodhue found much to admire in the Craftsman aesthetic and became cofounders of the Boston Society of Arts and Crafts, in 1908. Goodhue designed several impressive Spanish Colonial Revival-style buildings for San Diego's Panama-California Exposition of 1915, including the California Building, Balboa Park, which is now the Museum of Man. Shortly thereafter, the residential Pueblo Revival style overtook much of the Southwest.

Architect Irving J. Gill was another early Modernist who had trained with Louis Sullivan and moved into new building methods and materials that focused on integrating house and site. His Lewis Courts apartment building in Sierra Madre, California (1910), was a successful experiment in low-cost, hygienic housing, and his work with tilt-slab concrete construction resulted in the 1912 Banning House in Los Angeles and the Women's Club at La Jolla (1913). His best-known concrete house was designed for Walter Luther Dodge in 1916, but has since been demolished.

Other popular houses of the early- to mid-twentieth century include those in the Art Moderne Style (called Art Deco in commercial and public buildings). The style originated in Europe and received its first U.S. publicity in 1922, when the young Finnish architect Eliel Saarinen submitted an Art Deco design in the international competition held by the Chicago *Tribune* for a new headquarters building. It was widely admired by American architects and took second place in the competition. A year later, Eliel Saarinen emigrated to the United States and established his influential school of art and design, the Cranbrook Academy of Art, in Bloomfield Hills, Michigan. At the same time, stylish Art Moderne houses, influenced by the streamlined look of new trains, cars, and planes, sprang up across North America until the early 1940s. They had smooth walls, often faced with stucco; flat roofs with a small ledge, or coping, at the roofline; and little patterning apart from horizontal grooves. The corners of the building were often rounded, and glass blocks were used around window and door openings.

By the early 1920s, the parameters of Modern architecture had been established by four architects on two continents: Frank Lloyd Wright in the United States; the Swiss-born Le Corbusier, working in France; and Germany's Walter Gropius and Mies van der Rohe, both of whom would come to America during the political upheavals of the 1930s. The German architects were motivated by the quest for a pure form, which resulted in the Bauhaus—the school of design founded by Gropius in Dessau in 1919. Its official name was the *Staatliches Bauhaus* (State Building School), and its design was a new statement of the principle that the underlying structure should be visible. The construction materials were glass, steel, and concrete, and the façade formed a glazed extension from the steel supports that allowed for maximum interior light. The building was a study in clarity, precision, and symmetry, and the principles it embodied would be defined by Henry-Russell Hitchcock and architect Philip C. Johnson as the International style. Although he had been instrumental in the evolution of the style, with his rectilinear,

Below: A handsome bungalow influenced by the Arts and Crafts aesthetic: the Talcott House (1924), in Olympia, Washington.

Below: A remarkable art-glass tree design, continuous between redwood door panels and transom, at the Greene brothers' David B. Gamble House in Pasadena, California (1908).

hard-edged early work, Wright disavowed the International style and never acknowledged any influence on his work except Sullivan (although Japanese and pre-Columbian elements were clearly apparent in his later period).

Mies was the son of a master mason, and he once stated that "Architecture begins when you place two bricks *carefully* together." In 1905 he left his native

Aachen for Berlin, where he worked for architect and furniture designer Bruno Paul. There he learned another axiom that became well known: "A chair is a very difficult object to design. A skyscraper is almost easier; that is why Chippendale is famous."

In the Berlin office of architect Peter Behrens, Mies worked with both Le Corbusier and Walter Gropius and was influenced by the Neoclassic buildings of Carl Friedrich Schinkel. His 1923 design for a Brick Country House showed his growing concern with spatial relationships. According to Paul Heyer, in *Architects on Architecture* (Penguin Press, 1967): "Its brick walls supported the roof, while the overlapping planes articulated a subtle sequence of flowing space." His work was consonant with the principles of the Dutch *de Stijl* group, which united art and architecture within a single aesthetic.

After succeeding Gropius as the director of the Bauhaus in 1930, Mies faced increasing political interference and closed the school in 1933 to move to the United States. Gropius had accepted a position there as the head of Harvard University's Graduate School of Design, where he would have a revolutionizing influence on architectural education across North America. Mies established himself in Chicago, where he developed a master plan for the Illinois Institute of Technology's (originally the Armour Institute) 110-acre campus. His pre-eminence in the architecture of steel and glass became apparent in I.I.T.'s buildings and in his residential designs, including the Farnsworth House in Plano, Illinois (1950). This is a series of open planes and platforms that appears to float above its site. The interior service core separates

living and sleeping areas, which are flexibly defined by a series of panels. The house was in total contrast to the many period styles that had come into vogue again during the 1920s and '30s, and some critics resisted the growing influence of the International style most vehemently. H.H. Mencken protested that "If I were building a house tomorrow, it would certainly not follow the lines of a dynamo or a steam shovel….To say that the florid chicken coops of Le Corbusier and company are closer to nature than the houses of the eighteenth century is as absurd as to say that tar paper shacks behind the railroad tracks are closer to nature."

Its many critics notwithstanding, the International style was here to stay for decades to come, although its influence is more apparent in urban skyscrapers and complexes than in everyday residential architecture. The years following World War II are beyond the scope of this volume, which closes with the work of the European-born architects who came to North America as pioneers of the International style. They include, besides Mies and Gropius, the Viennese architects Rudolph Schindler and Richard Neutra, and German-born Marcel Breuer. Both Schindler and Neutra worked in southern California, where the way to innovation had been paved by Irving Gill. Neutra's best-known works include the stark multilevel Lovell House in Los Angeles (1928), which resembles a factory in its functional severity, and Schindler's Oliver House (1933), also in Los Angeles, with its flat roof and asymmetrical stairways and entry ramps, which are treated as ancillaries to the regularity of the primary forms.

After 1922 there were few fundamental changes in the International style, but the second generation of American architects trained by the European émigrés began to incorporate materials indigenous to their sites — native fieldstone, cedar roofing, and other elements that moved away from the concept of the house as "a machine for living" toward greater comfort and flexibility. This process has continued to unfold in the Postmodern era, reflecting the truth of Alfred North Whitehead's observation that "The art of progress is to preserve order amid change and to preserve change amid order."

Above: Early Modern design imbued with classical elements marks Eliel Saarinen's campus for the Cranbrook Academy of Art (1920s) in Bloomfield Hills, Michigan. Here the gifted émigré from Finland created a beautiful venue for the integrated study of the fine and design arts.

Bold Cantilevered Planes

Two of Wright's most striking cantilever designs are
seen at his home/studio Taliesin (above) in Spring Green,
Wisconsin, and the landmark house Fallingwater (opposite), designed for Edgar J. Kaufmann, Sr., in the western Pennsylvania highlands (1935). At Taliesin, the
cantilevered Birdwalk thrusts out into space from the
hilltop living room, with its bands of casement windows.
The soaring cantilevered balconies at Fallingwater alternate with walls and piers of native sandstone to form a
seamless union of house and site.

Sullivanesque Ornamentation   *Previous pages*

Louis Sullivan's rare gift for naturalistic ornament is
clear in these details from two of his works outside
Chicago: (page 228) the Peoples Savings & Loan Bank
in Sidney, Ohio (1917); and (page 229) the national
Farmers Bank in Owatonna, Minnesota (1907). His
love of design and structure would mature throughout
his career, resulting in his posthumous recognition as
the progenitor of Modern architecture.

Eliel Saarinen, Home/Studio *Overleaf*

The young Finnish architect Eliel Saarinen was already well known in Europe before he came to America. He designed the elegant brick Saarinen House (page 234) in 1930 at his newly founded Cranbrook Academy of Art in Bloomfield Hills, Michigan. His training in both architecture and painting made this home/studio an exemplar of early Modern design and a gathering place for artists of renown. The spare, uncluttered lines of the living room (page 235) show the influence of the notable Finnish architect Alvar Aalto (1898–1976).

The Wright/Sullivan Connection

Sullivan's influence on his chief draftsman during their six-year association (1887–93) is apparent in Wright's 1895 design for the Nathan G. Moore House (opposite) in Oak Park, Illinois. The client wanted a house in the newly fashionable Tudor Revival style (which Wright deplored), but his interpretation was uniquely his own, as seen in the rich gable woodwork, panel insets, and geometric balustrades (detail below) half enveloped in intricate reliefs.

Modernist Hallmarks

One sees clear affinities between the Saarinen House dining room above (restored 1996) and Frank Lloyd Wright's office in the Oak Park home/studio (right). The themes include effective use of art glass, geometrically patterned textiles, organic motifs drawn from nature, and fluid furniture designs intrinsic to their settings.

Framing the Landscape

Modern rooms with a view: (Opposite) Frank Lloyd Wright's beautiful living room for the landmark Meyer May House, designed in 1908 for a wooded site in Grand Rapids, Michigan, with elegant art-glass windows and coffered ceiling lights; (above) Eero Saarinen's Miller House, overlooking Ontario's Lake Rosseau, with natural stonework, burnished woods and metalwork, and subdued lighting that enhances rather than overpowers this natural setting in the Musoka Lakes region.

The Greene Brothers

The meticulous craftsmanship of architects Charles S. and Henry M. Greene made their California houses a byword for understated elegance. Above is the dining room of the David B. Gamble house in Pasadena (1908), which is reminiscent of Wright's Prairie style in its flow of living space from one area to another. The Japanese element is paramount in this "ultimate bungalow," whose living room (right) is a study in rich hand-carved red-wood and mahogany, with furniture and fixtures designed by the architects.

Essays in Stone

Michigan architect and builder Earl A. Young created many unique houses in his native Charlevoix, bordering Lake Michigan, during the 1930s and '40s. Each house was designed to fit its site, utilizing various types of stone—local quarry limestone, boulders, fieldstone, and others—with distinctive fireplaces, chimneys, and sloping cedar-shake roofs. In the example opposite, the masonry has been laid up in narrow courses to simulate natural formations; the house above is constructed mainly of boulders, with an irregular curved roofline that contributes to the sense of shelter.

Southwest Modernism

Traditional forms were reworked in new materials, including poured concrete, by architects like Irving Gill, who did many designs for clients in southern California. The striking terraced house on the opposite page, in Vickridge, Colorado, combines native and manmade materials with architectural plant forms to achieve its impressive effect. Below, the traditional bay window with balcony above, and the stepped entryway with decorative overhang, are freshly interpreted in a Pacific Palisades, California, home.

The All-American Bungalow

The single-story and multilevel bungalow were both built nationwide during the early twentieth century, with any number of regional variations. The Neuffer House (right), built in Olympia, Washington, in 1906, shows the influence of the Craftsman style in the Pacific Northwest, while the more contemporary version shown above freely combines traditional and modern forms to excellent effect on a hillside site in Sutter Creek, California.

Expressionism at Play *Overleaf*
The delightful Miller House (interior, page 239), by Eero Saarinen, is a postwar design incorporating vernacular elements from an earlier day, including flaring shingled rooflines supported by diagonal bracing, multi-textured wall surfaces, small-paned and diamond-paned windows, and extensive balustrades uniting the lakeside and its informal terraced approach. Resisting the dictates of the severe International style, Eero Saarinen and his father and colleague Eliel Saarinen, along with other European-American architects, experimented with the freedom to express their ideas in forms related to local geography, climate, and materials.

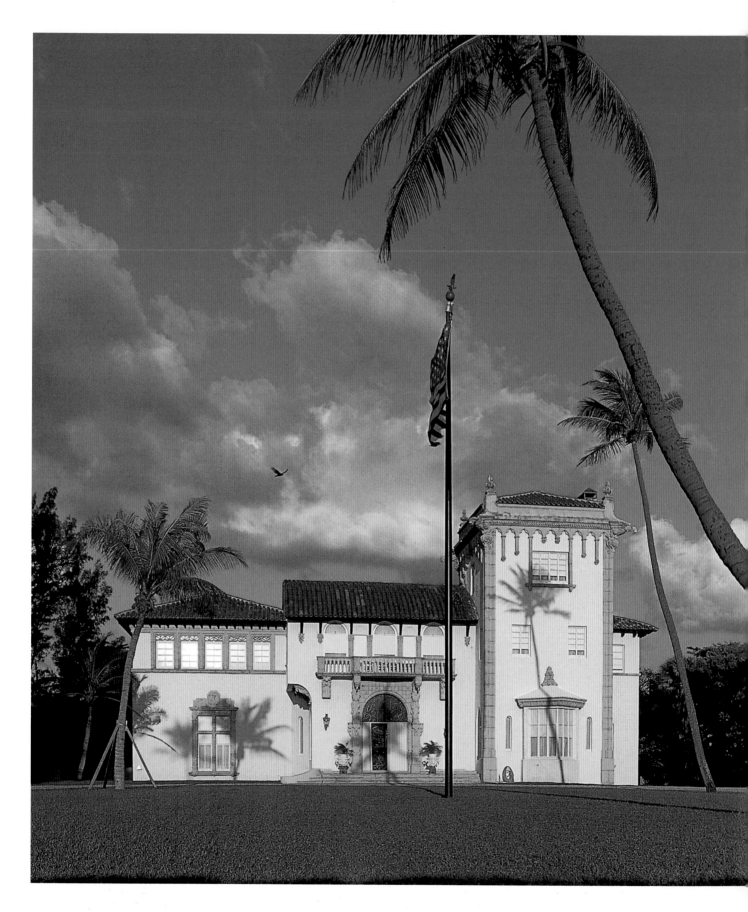

Floridian Styles

With the help of Henry Flagler's railroad and financing, Florida developed rapidly from one of the nation's least-populated areas into a mecca for builders and buyers during the early twentieth century. The state's benign climate, and extensive coastlines on both the Atlantic Ocean and the Gulf of Mexico, lent themselves to Mediterranean and Spanish-style houses like *Nuestro Paradisio* (Our Paradise), at left, designed by Julius Jacobs for a Palm Beach County client in 1928.

On Miami Beach (above), streamlined Art Deco apartment houses and hotels in a rainbow of pastel colors sprang up to accommodate winter-weary Northerners dazzled by the city's white sands and stylish buildings.

GLOSSARY

adobe Sun-dried clay bricks used for building in warm dry climates.

appliqué An ornament fastened to the surface of a building.

arcade A passageway with a roof supported by arched columns.

ashlar Smooth square-cut stone laid in horizontal courses with vertical joints.

bargeboard Projecting boards, usually decorated, placed on the **gable** ends of a house.

Baroque A post-Renaissance style characterized by ornate decoration, curvaceous forms, and complex compositions.

batten A narrow strip of wood used in alternation with wider vertical boards to weatherproof the seams of a building (called board-and-batten).

belt course A change of exterior masonry or patterning used to articulate the stories of a building; also called a stringcourse.

broken pediment A pediment in which one or both **cornices** are not continuous.

capital The top part of a column, usually decorated, and larger than the column shaft.

cantilever A projecting beam that is supported at only one end to form, e.g., a balcony.

cladding A finishing material, like boards or shingles, overlaid on an unfinished wall or roof as weatherproofing.

clapboard A thin board laid horizontally and overlapped to form a weathertight surface on a wooden building.

closed-string stairway One in which the balusters do not rest upon the treads, but upon a slanting footrail.

console An ornamental bracket for supporting a shelf, bust, cornice, etc.

corbel A masonry block projecting from a wall to support a horizontal feature.

cornice A projecting feature, usually decorative, at the top of walls, arches, and **eaves**.

crenellation Notched rooflines of medieval origin, also called battlements for their original defensive function.

dado The lower part of an interior wall when decorated differently from the upper part, as with panels or an ornamental border.

dentil One of a series of small rectangular blocks forming a molding, or projecting beneath a **cornice**.

dormer An upright window that projects from a sloping roof; may be gabled, shedlike, hipped, eyebrow-shaped, etc.

eaves The lower edge of a roof that projects beyond the wall below.

entablature The horizontal upper section of a classical **order**, resting on the **capital** and including the architrave, **frieze**, and **cornice.**

fanlight A fan-shaped window or transom over a door.

fenestration The arrangement of the windows and/or doors of a house.

flue An enclosed passage, as in a chimney, for conveying smoke, hot air, or other exhaust outside a building. A chimney often has several flues.

fretwork An ornamental feature consisting of three-dimensional geometric designs or other symmetrical figures (frets) enclosed in a band or border.

frieze A decorative band around a wall.

gable The triangular portion of an end wall below a ridged roof.

gambrel roof A ridged roof with two slopes on each side, the lower slope having the steeper pitch. Often seen on barns and neo-Dutch Colonial buildings.

gingerbread Ornate wooden decoration used on Victorian-style buildings.

half-timbering A type of construction in which spaces formed by a timber frame are infilled with stone, brick, stucco, or wattle and daub, leaving part of the frame exposed.

hipped roof One on which the external angle is formed by the meeting of two adjacent sloping sides.

hood molding An ornamental surround framing the upper part of a window.

modillion Plain rectangular supports below a **cornice** line indicating an extension of rafters through the wall.

mullion A vertical bar between the panes of a window.

order Columns or pilasters in various Greco-Roman styles, including Doric, Ionic, and Corinthian.

pediment A low triangular element, framed by horizontal sloping **cornices**, originating in Greek architecture and widely used as a design feature in Classical buildings, e.g., over doorways and windows.

parquet floor A floor covering of hardwood blocks laid in geometric patterns.

pendant A gable ornament suspended from the roof peak, often flanked by **bargeboards.**

pier A supporting post, usually square, shorter and thicker than a column.

pilaster A shallow columnlike feature attached to a wall and often used to frame doorways and fireplaces.

quoin A rectangle of stone, wood, or brick used in vertical series to decorate building corners and façade openings.

rococo French style developed from the Baroque, using elaborate ornamentation imitating foliage, rockwork, shellwork, scrolls, etc. and done with great delicacy and refinement.

segmental arch One composed of less than half a circle, used over windows, doorways, etc. as an ornament.

sidelights Narrow windows flanking a doorway.

stickwork The exterior patterned woodwork that serves an ornamental rather than a structural purpose; widely used in Victorian-style houses.

stucco A durable finish for exterior walls, usually composed of cement, sand, and lime.

tympanum Recessed space enclosed by the slanting **cornices** of a **pedi-**

ment; also, semicircular space enclosed by an arch over the top of a door.

vault An arched (domed) roof or ceiling.

wainscoting The woodwork that panels the lower portion of a room.

voussoir A wedge-shaped stone or brick used to form ornamental patterns on facades; also called a tab.

wattle and daub A building material composed of mud, stones, and sticks, used as infill between timber framing.

witch's cap A shingled, conical tower roof.

BIBLIOGRAPHY

Burnham, Alan, ed. *New York Landmarks: A Study & Index of Architecturally Notable Structures in Greater New York*. Middletown, Conn.: Wesleyan Univ. Press, 1963.

Colonial Williamsburg Foundation, The. *Legacy from the Past: A Portfolio of Eighty-eight Original Williamsburg Buildings*. Williamsburg, Va.: TCWF, 1971.

Cromie, Alice. *Restored Towns and Historic Districts of America*. N.Y.: E.P. Dutton, 1979.

Folsom, Merrill. *Great American Mansions and Their Stories*. Mamaroneck, N.Y.: Hastings House, 1963.

Foreman, John, and Robbe Pierce Stimson. *Vanderbilts and the Gilded Age, The Architectural Aspirations, 1879–1901*. N.Y.: St. Martin's Press, 1991.

Heyer, Paul, ed. *Architects on Architecture: New Directions in America*. London: Penguin Press, 1967.

Iovine, Julie V. "Mission Accomplished," *Metropolitan Home*, Nov. 1991.

Massey, James C., and Shirley Maxwell. *House Styles in America*. N.Y.: Penguin Books USA, 1996.

Packard, Robert, and Balthazar Korab. *Encyclopedia of American Architecture*, 2nd ed. N.Y.: McGraw-Hill, 1995.

Stewart, Doug, and Cameron Davidson. "Our Love Affair with Lawns," *Smithsonian*, Jan. 1999.

Walker, Lester. *American Shelter: An Illustrated Encyclopedia of the American Home* Woodstock, N.Y.: Overlook Press, 1981.

Waterhouse, P. Leslie, and R.A. Cordingley. *The Story of Architecture*. London: B.T. Batsford Ltd., 1950.

Whitehead, Russell F., Frank C. Brown, et al. *Survey of Early American Design*, Architectural Treasures of Early America series. N.Y.: The Early American Society/Arno Press, 1977.

INDEX

Page numbers in **boldface** refer to captions and illustrations.

Aalto, Alvar 233
Abbey, The **207**
Acadia *see* Canada, Atlantic
Adam style 26, 31, 113, **131**
Adam, James 10, 31
Adam, Robert 10, 31
Adam, William 31
Adler, Dankmar 222
Aesthetic Movement 116
Africa 84
Alabama: Demopolis 110–111; Turner 124
Alaska, Ketchikan 174–175
Alberta 15, 85, 151
Albert, prince of Saxe-Coburg 184
Amanites, the 82, 87
Ames estate **121**
Amish, the 87
Amstel House 18
"appleboard" **25**
architectural influences: 61; African 84; American 19, 117; Anglo 149; Canadian 12, 150; Caribbean 148; Creole 18; education and 226; English 8–9; Egyptian 18; French 14; German 60, 68, 87; Haitian 84; Japanese 224, 240; Mediterranean 59, 124, **138–139**, 148–149, 250–251; Mexican 137, 149; Modern 149, 222–226, **227**, 230, **244–245**; Native American 15, 149; "organic architecture" 223; postmodern 227; Southwestern 22, 85–86; Spanish 14–15, 58–59, **138–139**, 148, 250–251, (Moorish) 18, **64**, 115, **138–139**; Swiss 60, 87
Arizona: 86; Lee's Ferry 92–93
Arnold House, Christopher 17
Art Deco style 23, 149, 225, **251**
art-glass design **226**
Art Moderne style 225
Art Nouveau 116, **126**
Arts and Crafts Movement 20, 22, 116, 124, 183, 223
Ashbee, C.R. 223
Asher, Benjamin 30
Audubon, John James 148
Austin, Henry 184
Avenue of Oaks **118–119**

Banning House 225
Barbour, Governor James 30
Battle of Germantown, the 67
Bauhaus, the 225–226
Bay of Fundy 79
Beaux-Arts style 19, 31, 115, **115**, 116, **130–131**
Bedford Historic Village **80–81**
Behrens, Peter 226
Behunin Cabin 92
Bellingrath, Walter D. 124; estate **124**
Beringer, Frederick 127

Big Bend National Park **94**
Biltmore **136**
Bird, Joseph 159
Blacker House, Robert R. 22–23
Bok, Edward 22, 223
Boone Hall Plantation 118–119
Boston Society of Arts and Crafts, the 224
Bourn, William, Jr. 124
"Bourn Cottage" **124–125**
Braddock Hotel 18
Brandenburg Ranch House **163**
Breakers, the 19, 115, **132**
Bremond House, John, Jr. **115**
Breuer, Marcel 227
Brick Country House, the **226**
British Columbia: Vancouver 151; Victoria **44–45**, 151
Brooks Farm **47**
Bryant, William Cullen 188
Bulfinch, Charles 31, 113
Bungalow style **22**, 23, 149, **161**, 224, **225**, **240–241**, **246–247**
Burnham, Daniel H. (architect) 222

California: **36–37**, 85, 96, 116, 227; Amador County 158–159; Avalon **20**; Bodie **6–7**, **106–107**; Calaveras County **95**; Eureka **216–217**; Fall River Valley **178–179**; Ferndale **192–193**, **208**; Jackson 23; La Jolla 225; Los Angeles 23, 225, 227; Monterey 86; Moss Valley 117; Napa Valley **126**; Nevada County **124–125**; Nordhoff 224; Oakhurst 149; Pacific Palisades **245**; Pasadena 64, 224, **226**, **240**; St. Helena **212**; San Diego **62–63**, 224; San Francisco **130–131**, **180–181**, 184, 186, **218–219**; San Simeon 117; Santa Rosa **154**; Sierra Madre 225; Sonoma County **204–205**, **213**; Sutter Creek **182**, **246**; Trinity Alps **172**; Volcano **161**
Cameron House, J. Donald **195**
Campobello Island **78–79**
Campo Seco **95**
Canada: **88–89**, 185, 187; Atlantic 27, 43, 150; British 29; Eastern 9, 61, 113; French 112 *see also* Alberta, British Columbia, Manitoba, New Brunswick, Newfoundland, Nova Scotia, Ontario, Prince Edward Island; Quebec, Saskatchewan, Yukon Territory
cantilever design **230**
Canterbury Shaker Village **102–103**
Capitol Reef National Park 92, **98–99**
Carlyle House 18

Carpenter Gothic style 19, 114, **188**, **191**, **206**
Carson, William M. 216
Casa de Estudillo **62–63**
Celtic style 150
Central Park, N.Y.C. 137
Chalet style 18, **58**, **157**
Chalfin, Paul 134
Champlain, Samuel de 150
Charnley House 21, **222**, 222
Chateauesque style 16, 116, 133, **136**
Chateau Ramezay 56
Chipstone **41**
Choate House **37**
Church of England, the 86
Circle Meadow **96**
"City of Gold" **164–165**
Classicism **182–183**, 187; Jeffersonian 9, 26, 30, 112
Cloverdale Ranch **85**
Colonial style: 79, 124; Dutch 13–14, 57; English 8–9, 26; French 58, **75**, 148; New England **84**; Plantation 112; Revival 10, 19, **46**, 116, Spanish 15, 19, 59, 148–149, 85–86, 116, 149, 224
Colorado: Alta Mines **169**; Ashcroft **144–145**; Colorado Springs **22**; Georgetown **204–205**; Telluride **170–171**
Colross House 18
columns: Corinthian 113; Doric 75; Ionic 113
Connecticut: Norwalk 114; Stonington **52**; Westport **190**
construction/technique: adobe 59; all-wood 58; materials for 9, 59, 187, 225; stonework (masonry) **66–67**, 84–85, 87, 112, 187, **242–243**
Coonley House, Avery 222
Cordingley, R.A. 113
cottage style: 26, **36–37**, **69**; Cape Cod 12; cell-type 82; clapboard **38**; "Creole" style 56, 86, **160**; English 146; fieldstone-and-cedar 57; Gothic-style **155**; thatched-roof **45**, 59; urban 14
"Craftsman Homes" *see* Bungalow style
Cram, Ralph Adams 224
Cranbrook Academy of Art 23, 225, **227**, 233
Craftsman style 22, 246
Cubitt, Thomas 184

Dade County Art Museum 134
Davis, Alexander Jackson 19, 113–114, 137, 184
Deering, James 134
De La Salle Mansion **140**
Delaware, New Castle 18
Delaware (River) Valley 67
Destrehan Plantation **75**
details/ornamentation 57, **208**, **233**
District of Columbia, Washington **66**, 112
Dodge, Walter Luther 225
dogtrot cabin, the 82, **100–101**
Donnelly House **1**

Downing, Andrew Jackson 19–20, 113–114, 184, 186
du Calvet House, Pierre **13**, **73**
Dutch style 18, 57

Eclectic design 117
Eastlake, Charles 115
"Eastlake" style 115, **208**
École de Beaux Arts 115, 137, 184
Elfreth's Alley **50**
Elizabethan era 21
Enchanted Valley Chalet **173**
England: 31, 59; Kent 21; London 28, 183
English Gothic House 114
English-style manor house **124–125**
Ethnic Settlement Trail, the 82
Exotic Revival styles 18, 115

Fachwerk 13, 60
Fairfax House 18
Fallingwater 117, 223, **231**
false-front structure, the 147
Farmers Bank **229**
farmhouses: **31**, **67**; Dutch 57; Flemish 58; German **61**; masonry **47**; New England 27
Farnsworth House, 226
Federal style 10, 16, **24–25**, 26, 30, 48, **50–51**, 113
Finland 227
"first frontier" **83**
Flagler Museum, Henry Morrison 119, **134**, 251
Flemish style 112, **140**
Florida: 148; Key West 151; Miami Beach **135**, 251; Mount Dora **1**; Palm Beach 119; St. Augustine 58–59, 148
folk house **10**, 15
Ford, Henry 165
Fortress Louisbourg 150
Fowler, Orson Squire 113, 115
France: 58; Nimes 30; Paris 185
Francisco Terrace Apartments 223
French-Canadian style **68–71**
French Second Empire style 20, 115, 182, **184**, 185, 195
French Quarter, the **76–77**; 86, 148, **176–177**
frontier life 15, 59–61, 80–87
Furness, Frank 117

Gaineswood **110–111**
Gallagher House **184**
Gamble House, David B. 23, 224, **226**, **240**
Garden District, the **176–177**
Garden Suburb style 187
gargoyle 57
gatehouse, Fenno-Scandinavian 82
Geary House 212
Georgia: Atlanta **122**; Augusta 31; Helena 58; Savannah **11**, **18**, 20, 31, 113, **162**, **192**, 196

Georgian style 9, 17–18, 26–29, **30**, 33, 40, 112–113, 116 **194**; (Revival) **123**
Germany: Bavaria 32; Mainz 126
Gibbs, James 10
Gill, Irving J. 224, 227, 245
"gingerbread" *see* Carpenter Gothic
Gingerbread Mansion **208**
Glen Auburn **200–201**
Glenview House **203**
Glessner House, John 116
Goelet, Ogden 133
Goodhue, Bertram Grosvenor 224
Gothic Revival style 18–19, 113, **137**, 182, **195**, 224
Gramercy Park West **196–197**
Grand Hotel 212
Grand Portage National Monument **70–71**
Grant style, General U.S. 185
"Great American Desert" 84
Greco-Roman style 112, 182
Greek Revival style 10, 18, 31, **75**, **110–111**, 112–114, 116, 182
Greene, Charles 21–23, 224, 226, 240
Greene, Henry 21–23, 224, 226, 240
Gropius, Walter 225–227
Gunston Hall 112

"Habitation" 150
hacienda 86
Hall House, Joseph **191**
Hamilton House 17
Harris-Cameron House **192**
Harvard University 32, 226
Hathaway, Anne 45
Hausmann, Baron Georges-Eugene 20, 185
Hawaii: Niulii **108**; Oahu **146**
Hearst, William Randolph 117
Hemingway, Ernest 148
Heritage Village **82**
Herndon Home, the **122**
Herr House, Hans **68**
Herter, Gustav 185
Heurtley House, Arthur **224**
Heyer, Paul 226
Highland Gardens 114
High Victorian Gothic style 19, 115, **117**, 183, 186
Hildene **123**
Hill House, Holly **20**
Hill, Samuel 127
Hispano-Moorish style **142–143**
Hitchcock, Henry Russell 225
Hoban, James 19
Hoffman, F. Burrall, Jr. 134
hogans 147
Hopps House 117
"House of Four Seasons" **206**
Hubbard House **79**
Hudson (River) Valley 56–57, **203**
Hull-Barrow House 31
Hunt, Joseph H. 117
Hunt, Richard H. 117
Hunt, Richard Morris 18–19, 115, 117, 133, 137

Idlewild 114
Illinois: Chicago 183, 222–223; Highland Park 222; Oak Park 20, 186, 222, **223**, **232**, **236–237**; Plano 226; River Forest 222
Illinois Institute of Technology, the 226
immigrants/settlers: 61, 151; Amish 60; Anglo 85; Austrian 58; Cajun 86; Dutch 13–14, 56; English 151; French 14, 58, 150; German 13, 58, 68, 82, 84, 87; Mennonites 61, 87; Puritans 26; Scandinavian 84; Scots-Irish 13, 84; Spanish 59; Swedish 13, 82–83; Swiss 58; Ukrainian 85
Indiana 83, 87
"Inspirationists" *see* Amanites
International style 225–227, 247
Iowa: 87; Des Moines **21**; Urbandale **166**
Iron Master's House **8**
Italianate style 20, **21**, 113, 114, 137, 147, **183**, 184–185, **195**, **196–197**
Italy 115

Jackson, President Andrew 148
Jacobean style 10, 17, 21, 112
Jacobs, Julius 251
Japanese teahouse, the 224
Jay, William 31, 113
Jefferson, Thomas 10, 16, 19, 30, 112
Jenney, William Le Baron 222
Johnson, Philip C. 225
Jones, Inigo 10, 29

Kahn, Alfred 23
Kansas 82
Kaufmann, Edward J., Sr. 117, 230
Keiller House **43**
Kentucky 82–83, 137
Kerr, Robert 183
Kresge Foundation 46

Lake House **183**
Lane House, Job **34**
Laramore-Lyman House **149**
Larkin, Thomas O. 149
Latrobe, Benjamin H. 19, 113, 182
Laura Plantation House **160**
Le Corbusier, Charles 225–227
Lewis Courts apartments 225
Libby, Joseph R. 184
Lienau, Detlef 114
Lincoln Log toy house 147
Lincoln Pioneer Village 83
Lincoln, Robert Todd 121
Living History Farm, the 21
Lockwood-Mathews Mansion **114**
log cabin/house styles 13, **15**, 60, 82–84, **86**, **88–89**, 91, **96–97**, **104–109**, 147, **157**, **159**; "mossback" 83; shingle-roofed **90**
Longwood 115, **117**

Louisiana: **83**; New Iberia 74–75; New Orleans 14, **76–77**, 84, 86, 148, **176–177**; St. Francisville **4**; Vacherie **160**; White Castle **116**
Lovell House 227
Luna's Jacal **94**
Lyndhurst 19, 114, **137**

Magnolia Plantation **83**
Maine: 17, **28**, 79; Portland 184; Rockport **215**; Wicasset 31
Maison Carrée, the 30
maison de ville **72**
maison traditionelle (French Colonial) 58
Manitoba 85, **91**, 151
Mansart, François 20
mansion, the 10–11, 110–143
Mar-a-Lago (Sea to Lake) **142–143**
Marble House 19
Martinez Adobe **147**
Martin House, Darwin 222
Mary Hill Museum of Art **128–129**
Maryland: 61; Baltimore **51**
masonry houses 29, 48–49, **124–125**, 147, 187
Massassachusetts: 10, 86, **102–103**; Bedford **34**; Beverly 48; Boston 31, 113, 116, 184; Cape Cod 12; Deerfield 30; Ipswich 26, **37**; Martha's Vineyard **188**; Nantucket Island 27; North Easton **121**; Plymouth 26, **53**; Salem 30, 113; Saugus **8**; Stockbridge **33**; Waltham 16; Woburn **35**;
Maybeck, Bernard 117
May House, Meyer **237–238**
McIntire, Samuel 16, 30, 113
Medford Farmhouse, the **32**
medieval style **8**, 58
Mencken, H.H. 227
Mercer House **196**
Michigan: Bloomfield Hills 23, **220–221**, 225, **227**, **234**; Charlevoix 243; Grand Rapids **237–238**; Greenfield Village **167**; Mackinac Island **189**, **210–211**; Troy **47**
Mies van der Rohe, Ludwig 225–27
Miller House **239**, **248–249**
Mills, Robert 19
Minnesota: **70–71**; Minneapolis **140–141**; Owatonna 229
Mission House **33**, 212
Mission style 59, 116
Mississippi, Natchez **60**, 115, **117**, **200–201**
Mississippi (River) Valley 58
Missouri, Boonville **198–199**
Monterey style 86, 149, **161**
Monticello 17, 31, **112**, 112
Moore House, Nathan G. **232**
"Moravian Castle" **17**
Morgan, Julia 117
Morgan Library, J. Pierpont 116
Mormons, the 82, 92
Morris, William 116, 124
Morse-Libby House 184
Morse, Ruggles S. 184

Moses, Simon 200
Mount Baker **103**
Mount Vernon 9, 17, 31, 112
Museum of American Frontier Culture 61, **87**
Museum of Man and Nature 91

Napoleon III, emperor of France 20, 185
Navajo, the 147
Nebraska 84
Neoclassical style 31, 113, 226
Nesfield, Eden 21
Neuffer House **246–247**
Neutra, Richard Joseph 23, 227
Nevada: Nye County **85**; Reno 183
New Amsterdam 57
New Brunswick: 79; 150; Dorchester **43**
New England style 12, 61
Newfoundland: 151; Fogo Island **38**; Hart's Cove **39**
New France 58 *see also* Canada, Eastern
New Jersey: 58; Cape May **184**, 185, **191**, **207**, 209
New Mexico 59, 86; Pueblo Bonito **59**; Taos **147**
New York: 57, 86, 184; Buffalo 222; East Aurora 22, 223; Easthampton **33**; Mount Lebanon **84**; Newburgh **29**, 114; New York City **65**, 116, 137, **196–197**; Rose Valley 22, 223; Syracuse 22; Tarrytown 19, 114, **137**
Nichols-Sortwell House 31
Nightingale, Colonel Joseph 17
Norman style 116
North Africa 59
North Carolina: 61; Asheville **136**
North Dakota 84
North Evans Chateau **133**
Notman, John 115
Nottaway **116**
Nova Scotia: 150; Blomidon **168–169**
Nuestro Paradisio **250–251**

Oahu, Laie **146**
Octagonal house, the 18, 115, **117**
Ohio: 87; Sidney **228–229**
Ojibwa, the 68
Olde England Inn, the **44–45**
Old Town Historic District **62–63**
Oliver House 227
Olmsted, Frederick Law 20, 137
Oneto House **158–159**
Ontario 151
Open Gates **199**
Oregon, Portland **16**, 120
Osborne House 184
Otis, Elisha Graves 222
"outshot" house 27
Owenites, the 82
Owens-Thomas House **11**

Pabst, Frederick 127; mansion **127**
Paine, Thomas 30
"Painted Ladies" 186, **208**
Palladian, Anglo- 113

Palladio 29, 31
Panama-California Exposition 224
pattern books 146
Paul, Bruno 226
Pennsylvania: 60, 82, 87, 90; Bank of 182; Bear Run 117, 223; Doylestown **17**; Harrisburg **194–195**; Lancaster County **68**; Philadelphia **50**, 61, 113, 117, 182–184; Pittsburgh 186; Virginville **46**; Worcester **67**
"Pennsylvania Dutch" style, the 56, 60–61, **68**
Peoples Savings & Loan Bank, the **228–229**
Pfeiffer's Homestead **2**
Pierce-Nichols House 30
Pingree House, Gardner 30
Pino-Charlet House 149
Pittock, Georgiana 120
Pittock, Henry 120
Pittock Mansion **16**, 120
plantation house 112, **116**, **118–119**
plaque, antique **3**
Plimouth Plantation **26**
Polk, William 124
Polynesian Cultural Center **146**
Ponce de Leon 58
Post, George Browne 117
Post, Marjorie Merriwether 141
Prairie House, the 21, 117, 222, **224**
Pratt House, Charles M. 224
Price, William 22, 223
Prince Edward Island: **27**, 151; Argyle Shores 148; North Wiltshire **155**; Souris **152–153**
Pueblo Revival style 59, 224
Pugin, Augustus W.N. 183

Quakers, the 84, 127
Quebec: 150; Montreal **13**, **56**, 58, **73**, 112, 185, **202**; Percè **54–55**; Rosemere 12, **69**
Queen Anne Revival style **1**, 18–19, **20**, 115, **180–181**, **185**, 186–187, **190**, **208**, **212**

ranch house, the 82
Red House, the (Bexleyheath) 21, 124
Regency style 26, 31, 113
Renaissance style: 9, 113, 182, 184; English 28; French 119 **119**, **120**, **134**; Italian 29, **116**, **132**, 184; (Revival) 18, 115–116
Rhine House, the **126**
Rhode Island: 11, 26, **187**; Newport 10, 17, 19, 115, **140**, **200**; Providence 17
Richardson, Henry Hobson 20, 116, 186, 224
Robie House 117, 223
Robins Villa 114
Rogers, George B. 124
Romanesque style 19–20, 113–114, **199**, (Richardsonian) 116, 186, 224

roofing/rooflines 57–58, 115, 185, **202**, **207**, (witch's cap) **185**, (mansard) **198–199**
Roosevelt, Franklin D. (summer house) **78–79**
Root, John W. (architect) 222
Rosedown **4**
Roycroft 22, 223
Ruskin, John 22, 183, 186
Ruskinian Gothic style *see* High Victorian

Saarinen, Eliel 23, 225, 227, 233, 247
Saarinen, Eero 23, 239, 247
Saarinen House **234**, **236**
saddlebag house, the 82
saltbox style 27, **27**, **32**, 151
Sanders Home, the **161**
Saskatchewan 85
Schindler, Rudolph 227
Schinkel, Carl Friedrich 226
Scott, Walter Perry 137
Scully, Vincent 185–186
Seghesio Winery **213**
Seminole, the 59
Sequoia National Park **96**
Shadows-on-the-Teche **74**
Shakers, the 82, 86–87
shanty, the 146
Shaw Island **108**
Shaw, Richard Norman 21, 186
Shingle style 20, 186, **187**
Short, Colonel Robert H. 176
"shotgun house" 84
Simonton Court **151**
slave quarters 82–84, **83**
Sloane, Samuel 115, 117
Smith House, Melvyn Maxwell **220–221**
Soane, John 31
South Carolina, Charleston **131**
South Dakota 84
"Southwestern" style 56
Spanish Baroque style 60
Spanish Town 149
Spreckels, Adolph 131
Staatliches Bauhaus see Bauhaus
stained glass **140–141**
Starrett House 206
State Building School *see* Bauhaus
Stewart-Dougherty House 149
Stickley, Gustav 22, 223
Stick style 18, 115, 185–186
Stockton Cottage **209**
stone-ender, the 26
Sullivan, Louis Henri 8, 21, 117, 222, 224, 226, 233
Sutter Home Winery **212**
Swiss chalet, the 146–147, 224

Talcott House **225**
Taliesin 230
Telfaire House 31
Tennessee 86
Territorial styles 86, 149
Texas 86, **94**; Austin 115, **133**; Fredericksburg **100**; Galveston 199; Hilda **163**; Independence **157**; Round Mountain **159**; Stonewall **100–101**
Thompson, Benjamin 32

Tift House, Asa 148
Tioronda 114
townhouses: **65**, **162**, **176–177**; **180–181**, **219**; early 57; Quebec-style masonry **13**, **14**, **56**, 58, **72–73**, 116, **202**
Trask, Oliver 48
Trinity Church 116
Trumbull House, Gordon **52**
Tudor Revival style 21, 116, **121**, **186**, 233
Turnblad, Swan J. 140
Tyson, Elise 17
Tyson, Emily 17

Upjohn, Richard 20, 113
Urban, Joseph 141
Usonian house, the 22
Utah: 92, **98–99**; Salt Lake

City 82
Utopian communities 82, 86–87, 223

Vale, the 16
Valley Forge National Historic Park 90
Vanderbilt, Cornelius II 19, 115, 133
Vanderbilt, George W. 137
Vaux, Calvert 20, 114, 137
Vermont: Manchester **123**; Weston **31**
vernacular styles 10–11, ("Old English") 21, 144–179
Vickridge **22**, **244**
Victoria, queen of Great Britain 184
Victorian era/style 18–19,

114, 180–219
Vieux Carrè see French Quarter
vigas 59, 85
Virginia: 30, 61, 113; Barboursville 30; Charlottesville 19; Jamestown 10; Mount Vernon **9**, 17, 31, 112; Richmond **40**; Staunton **61**, **87**
Vizcaya 134, **135**
Voysey, Charles F.A. 21, 223

Walker, Lester 112
Ware House, Nicholas 31
Washington: Goldendale 127; Hoquiam **185**; Olympia **225**, **246–247**; Olympic National Park

173; Port Townsend **206**; Seattle **150**
Washington, George 9, 16, 29, 31, 67, 12
Watch Hill **187**
Waterhouse, P. Leslie 113
Webb, Philip 21, 124
Weeks, David 75
Wentz, Peter 67
West Indies 131
whale house, Nantucket 27
Whipple House, John 26
"White City" 183
Whitehall **119**, **134**
Whitehead, Alfred North 227
White House, the 185
Whitfield, Nathan B. 112
Willits House, Ward W. 117, 222

Wilton **40**
Wisconsin: Fox Point **41**; Green Bay **82**, **214**; Hudson **113**; Milwaukee **127**; Pendarvis 84
Withers, F. Clarke 114
Women's Club, La Jolla 225
Wren, Christopher 10
Wright, Frank Lloyd 8, 20–21, 117, 183, 186, 222–226, 230, 233, 236
Wyeth, Marion Sims 141
Wyoming, Grand Teton **2**, **104–105**

Young, Earl A. 243
Yukon Territory, Dawson City **164–165**

ACKNOWLEDGMENTS

The publisher would like to thank the following individuals for their help in the preparation of this book: Nicola J. Gillies, managing editor; Sara Hunt, editor; Charles J. Ziga, art director and photographer; Nikki L. Fesak, graphic designer; Lisa Langone Desautels, indexer. The input of the following people was invaluable: Kelly C. Barr; A. Blake Gardner; Marilyn Holnsteiner; Marcie Johnson; Peter M. Manjuck, Patti Morcos, and Wayne A. DiGiacomo of Champion Printing; Annie Lise Roberts, architect; Elaine Rocheleau; Walter Christopher Wanzie.

PHOTO CREDITS

Grateful mention is made here of the talented men and women and photographic agencies whose work is featured on the following pages:
© **Theo Allofs:** 88–89, 97, 156, 166–67 (both); © **Larry Angier:** 36–37b, 59, 94, 98–99, 100, 176, 177; © **Peter Arnold, Inc:** 118–19b (© Clyde H. Smith); © **Tony Arruza:** 1, 142, 143, 250; © **Barett & MacKay Photo:** 26, 53; © **2000 Kindra Clineff:** 24–25, 30, 31, 33, 188; © **Janelco Photographers/Eliot Cohen:** 34, 35, 78–79 (both), 121, 140t; © **Ed Cooper Photo:** 6–7, 8, 9, 17, 29, 32, 70–71, 92–93 (both), 109, 128–29, 138–39, 144–45, 146, 149, 171r, 172–73, 175, 204, 205, 208, 212; © **D.E. Cox Photo Library/ChinaStock:** 189, 210–11, 243; © **Grace Davies:** 57, 65, 132; © **Carolyn Fox:** 23, 85, 95, 158–59l, 161, 182, 246t; © **Winston Fraser:** 12, 15, 54–55, 62–63 (both), 69, 91; © **Thomas Hallstein/Outsight:** 154, 174, 178–79, 213; © **Rudi Holnsteiner:** 58, 60, 68, 80–81, 83, 101, 115, 116, 117, 124t, 133, 136, 157, 159t, 160, 163, 198–99 (both), 200–201r; © **James Hyland:** 75, 112; © **Kerrick James:** 64, 180–81; © **Wolfgang Kaehler:** 2, 18, 104–105, 131t, 162; © **Balthazar Korab:** 22, 47, 66, 82, 113, 140–41b, 220–21, 222, 223, 227, 228, 229, 231, 234, 235, 236t, 238, 239, 240–41 (both), 242, 244, 248–49; © **Craig Lovell:** 16, 28, 76, 77, 106–107, 120, 164–65b, 169, 216, 217, 245; © **Chuck Pefley:** 10, 11, 21, 44–45 (both), 50, 51, 103, 108, 122, 150, 164t, 192t, 196t, 219; © **Chuck Place:** 20, 90, 96, 124–25b, 126, 130–31b, 147, 183, 185, 206, 207, 218, 226; © **Paul Rocheleau:** 4, 37t, 40, 41, 48t, 67, 74, 84, 86, 87, 102, 110–11, 119t, 123, 127, 134, 135, 151, 168, 192–93b, 230, 236–237r; © **Rob and Ann Simpson:** 61; © **John Sylvester:** 27, 38, 39, 42–43 (both), 148, 152–53, 155, 170–71l; © **Graeme Teague:** 251; © **Charles J. Ziga:** 3, 13, 46, 48–49b, 52, 56, 72, 73, 114, 137, 184, 186, 187, 190, 191, 194, 195, 196–97r, 200t, 202, 203, 209, 214, 215, 224, 225, 232, 233, 247b.